The Hindu Society of Alberta

A Fifty-Year History

The Hindu Society of Alberta
A Fifty-Year History

Deepro Chakraborty

The Hindu Society of Alberta

2019

Published by The Hindu Society of Alberta
14225–133 Avenue NW, Edmonton, Alberta T5L 4W3,
Canada.

http://www.hsa50.ca

First published 2019

© 2019 by The Hindu Society of Alberta

Book credits:
- Research and writing: Deepro Chakraborty
- Editor: Dr Laura Servage
- Cover design and creation: Shreela Chakrabartty
- Copyediting, text design and typesetting: Dominik Wujastyk

ISBN-13   978-1-9994314-0-2
          978-1-9994314-1-9 (ePDF)

Ordering information:
This book may be purchased online from Lulu.com. It is also distributed through other online book services such as Amazon and all good bookshops. Copies may also be ordered from the publisher, the Hindu Society of Alberta, at the address given above.

आ नो भद्राः क्रतवो यन्तु विश्वतः

Let noble thoughts come to us from every side

— Ṛgveda-saṃhitā 1.89.i

Contents

Foreword	i
Preface	iii
An Overview of the History of the Hindu Society of Alberta	1
Early Historical Background	6
Establishment of the HSA	8
The HSA: Before Its Cultural Centre	11
The Fabric of the HSA	15
The Hindu Cultural Centre	23
The Priest	40
The Kitchen	43
Activities and Services	44
Connection with Other Non-Governmental Organizations	58
Appendix A: Past Executives and Boards	60
Appendix B: Notable Figures and Contributors	86

Foreword

THE YEAR 2017 MARKED THE GOLDEN ANNIVERSARY of the Hindu Society of Alberta. The Society's Board decided to celebrate its 50th anniversary by recognizing the founding members at a special event for Diwali. To prepare for this event, I began an initial search for information about founding members at the Hindu Cultural Centre library, looking for any documents that would give us some information as to how it all began. After hours of searching I found information that gives us an understanding of the organization's early years. Herein, we learn how a few individuals with a clear vision carried on in face of the adversity to establish the Hindu Society of Alberta.

Once I began my inquiry, it was quickly evident that finding information about the expansion of the facility would be a task that would require persistence and many hours of hard work. Little did I know how challenging this task would become, or how interesting and enriching this historical journey would be. The reward of these efforts was learning about the long history of the Society's programming, and the many people who helped the Hindu Society of Alberta (henceforth HSA) to evolve into its present form: a gathering place for community members to worship, socialize, and participate in cultural activities.

Canada celebrated its 150-year Anniversary in 2017. Among many initiatives to mark the occasion, federal and provincial governments provided financial support to community organizations to help them plan their own celebratory and commemorative events. The Hindu Society of Alberta applied for funding and received $24,850 from the Province of Alberta to research and document the history of the organization. The process of application for funding was led by Mr Rajeev Arora, Vice President Communication of the Hindu Society of Alberta Board. My sincere thanks to Mr Arora for his advice throughout the project and his thoughtful contributions. In May of 2018, under the guidance of Dr Dominik Wujastyk, Professor and Singhmar Chair at the University of Alberta, Mr Deepro Chakraborty was hired to research and write the history of the Hindu Society of Alberta. Our sincere thanks to Mr Sushil Kumar Kalia for his advice, support and for his patience in answering our many questions throughout the project, to the Government of Alberta for the financial support, to Mr Deepro Chakraborty for undertaking the challenging task of compiling the history of the HSA, to all past and current HSA members who provided information to make writing of this book possible, Prof. Wujastyk for copy-editing, design and typesetting, to Shreela Chakrabartty for designing and creating the cover of the book and to editor Dr Laura Servage for her careful editing.

On behalf of the Hindu Society of Alberta Board, it is our hope that you will enjoy reading the historical account of the oldest Hindu cultural and religious organization in Edmonton.

Hansa Thaleshvar,
President 2016–2018

Preface

THE FIFTY-YEAR JOURNEY of the Hindu Society of Alberta exemplifies the organization-oriented religious life of the Hindus in western lands. Hinduism is a religion with a set of different beliefs originating on the Indian subcontinent. Although they emerged thousands of years ago out of simple pagan belief systems, Hindu philosophies have evolved refined positions on ontology (the understanding of the universe), epistemology (the understanding of knowledge) and soteriology (the understanding of the purpose of life)— all ranging from gross materialism to ultimate spiritualism, and from polytheism[1] to monotheism,[2] monism[3] and atheism. Modern Hindu practices consist of a more-or-less universal pantheon and certain socio-religious (Sanskrit: *dharmaśāstra*) injunctions. Between these positions, the practices and rituals among different regional and linguistic communities are highly diverse.

In India, Hindu religious life extends from family customs into temples dedicated to particular gods or goddesses, or to religious gatherings of a particular faith group, called *satsaṅga*s. The direct formation of non-political religious organizations under the umbrella term "Hindu" is a feature of the Hindu diaspora outside India. Despite tremendous differences in faiths and performances of rituals, the Hindu minority populations in foreign lands are characterized by a cultural intimacy that motivates them to form community organizations.

---

1. The belief in multiple divinities.
2. The belief in a single God.
3. The belief that everything is constituted of a single entity, in which God and the universe are the same.

It is always a challenge in such organizations to maintain a pan-Hindu character so that all members feel culturally included. The study of these organizations is, therefore, interesting from a sociological point of view. I am afraid I could not make my report a full exploration of such sociological insights and analysis. This publication is, rather, a collection of the factual details about the Hindu Society of Alberta which I was able to collect by looking at official documents and interviewing individuals who have been involved with the development of the Society as it stands today. I still hope that this narrative about the Hindu Society of Alberta (HSA), the oldest Hindu organization of Edmonton, will be useful to sociological researchers as a case study. It will also be useful as a historical record to members of the Society, and to those who would be interested to learn about it.

I am indebted to the Board of Directors of the HSA (2017–2018), to my advisor Prof. Dominik Wujastyk, in the Department of History and Classics, University of Alberta, and to Mrs Hansa Thaleshvar, President of the Society (2016–2018) for allowing me to do this work. Prof. Wujastyk introduced me to Mrs Thaleshvar who, in consultation with Mr Rajeev Arora, the Vice President (Communications) of the HSA, kindly hired me for this project on behalf of the Board. My work would never have been possible without the assistance of Mr Sushil Kumar Kalia, the honourary priest of the Society. He helped me with official documents which are, unfortunately, not in the Society's official archives.

As a newcomer to Canada, it was hard for me to learn about the local Hindu community and write the history of the Society. Ms Shreela Chakrabartty, another member of the Society, familiarized me with the Hindu community in Edmonton, offering her insights and other useful information. She also checked the whole document and made necessary suggestions. My sincere thanks go to Dr Laura Servage who thoroughly proofread and edited the report. I am also grateful to many other individuals who despite their busy schedules

Preface

helped me by answering my numerous queries. They are:

Dr Ram Krishan Gupta	Mr Balvant Gandhi
Dr Sujit Kumar Chakrabartty	Mr Pitambar Lal Avasthi
Ms Aruna Chakrabartty	Mr Amar Bhasin
Mr Prabhu Dayal Sarhadi	Mr Krishan Kumar Chawla
Dr Krishan Lal Katyal	Mrs Meera Mittra
Dr Reva Joshee	Mr Desh Mittra
Mrs Karuna Joshee	Mr Rajiv Ranjan
Mr Sushil Kumar Kalia	Mr Rajeshwar Singh
Mr Jivan Kayande	Dr Kamal Nath Jha
Mrs Maya Murdeshwar	Acharya Shiv Shankar Prasad Dwivedi
Mr Ramesh Chander Khullar	
Mrs Kamlesh Khullar	Mr Kartikeya Arora
Mr Preetam Sharma	Ms Rupam Arora
Mrs Sandhya Bagwe	

Without the valuable information they provided, I would never have been able to complete this project. *Vedanta and Hindu Diaspora in Canada,* a book by Dr Chakrabartty, was in many ways useful in my work, and in particular contains a chapter on the early history of the Society. I also used Dr Chakrabartty's documents related to the Society, which are held by the Provincial Archive of Alberta, in Edmonton.

Disclaimer: Everything in this report is from the official documents I could collect and the personal interviews. I had no connection with the Society before I began working on it in May 2018. Therefore, any overlooking or misrepresentation of facts is solely due to the limited information available to me.

— Deepro Chakraborty,
Edmonton, June 2019

An Overview of the History of the Hindu Society of Alberta

THE STORY OF THE HINDU SOCIETY OF ALBERTA is all about making a religious space for the Hindu diaspora in Edmonton. Over its fifty-year journey, we will see how similar religious affiliations attracted young, educated Hindus, and how they formed a community and eventually, a physical community centre. We will examine members' quests for scriptural, philosophical and cultural understanding, and how ritual performance was introduced into the HSA. Gradually, rituals changed the fundamental nature of the Cultural Centre, and consequently the Society attracted many new members. We will see how members raised funds and volunteered their time to improve the financial strength and stability of the Society, and how the Society has contributed to cultural understanding in Alberta over its fifty years.

In the second half of the twentieth century the Government of Canada relaxed strict immigration rules. The following years saw an influx of immigration. Many South Asians immigrated to Alberta at this time. Similar cultural and religious practices and ideology brought Hindu South Asians together in dense networks and close associations. Such informal bonding often provides the main impetus to create a formal community organization, and the Hindu Society of Alberta was no exception.

The earliest efforts to form the Society came from academicians, most of whom were professors or students at the University of Alberta. They were young enthusiasts who were curious about their cultural roots. Some of these early members had participated in or witnessed the establishment of formal organizations in other western countries and drew motivation from these experiences. Another stimulus came from Swami Bhashyananda, a Hindu monk of the Vivekananda Vedanta Society, who visited Edmonton in 1967 and delivered a lecture at the University of Alberta. He inspired the Hindus to establish a formal association.

On November 1, 1967, Dr Ram Krishan Gupta, a professor of educational psychology at the University of Alberta, formed the Hindu Society of Alberta (HSA) with thirty other founders whom he had invited to his house for the Diwali celebration. This was the inception of the first formal Hindu organization in Alberta. The members gave the Society a democratic shape through an elected organizing committee. They created a constitution, later supplemented with bylaws, which have been modified several times over the years. In 1972, the society was registered under the Society Act of Alberta.

The "movers and shakers" of the HSA during its early days were highly educated, including both faculty and students at the University of Alberta. They had broad visions, innovative ideas, and a thirst for knowledge and art. The major activities of the Society were weekly sessions of Hindu scripture discussions (usually the *Bhagavadgītā* and the *Rāmāyaṇa*), Indian language classes (Hindi and Bengali), cultural events for music and dance, screenings of Indian movies, and cultural festivals. Ritual worshipping was not an essential part of the Society's early activities.

Gradually, HSA membership increased. The Society received leased land from the provincial government on which to build its Cultural Centre. The Society later purchased the land. Some members proposed that in order to attract more people to the Society, they would need to perform religious ceremonies. This idea led members to establish a temple at the Cultural Centre, which was made functional in 1981 and formally inaugurated in 1984.

In the early 1980s, many affluent North Indian Hindus, especially Punjabis, who resided in and around Edmonton began coming to the Hindu temple of the Hindu Cultural Centre. They contributed to better attendance, healthy financing and enhanced programs. These new members were instrumental in serving shared meals after Sunday worship, and special *pūjā* (worship) in the temple. Their energy and enthusiasm made the HSA more vibrant, and the Society became stronger. Since this formative period, the activities of the HSA have transitioned to focus more on religious rites, worship, rituals and ceremonies than cultural events, although the HSA continues to host and participate in cultural and inter-faith events for the community.

Mr Sushil Kumar Kalia began volunteering as a priest of the temple in 1976. He introduced celebrations of various religious ceremonies and festivals, often in innovative ways and with an inclusive pan-Indian approach. In 1989, the society appointed Acharya Shiv Shankar Prasad Dwivedi as the permanent official priest. Acharya Dwivedi, a gold medalist in Sanskrit, had pursued traditional studies, learning Sanskrit and performance of Hindu religious ceremonies.

As the Society was growing, it required a larger and more stable source of funding. Initially, the Society raised funds mainly from donations and screenings of Indian movies. Mr Krishan Chandra Joshee, who was very influential in the higher levels of government and was a recipient of the Order of Canada, introduced the idea of participating in the bingos and casinos. He also helped the society to obtain various government grants. Since the 1980s, the Society began volunteering with the gaming industry and it became the main source of funding.

Over its fifty-year history, the HSA has positively influenced the growth and vibrancy of Edmonton's Hindu community. At the time of its inception, the HSA was the first Hindu organization in Edmonton. Today there are several Hindu organizations and temples across the city. These reflect different linguistic, ethnic and cultural identities of Hindus, and differences in religious outlooks and pursuits. The growing number of Hindu immigrants in the city and the inconvenience of the Cultural Centre's north side location for residents in south Edmonton were contributing factors to the establishment of other Hindu organizations and temples. The South Indian and Sri Lankan Hindus prefer to go to the temples of the Maha Ganapathy Society or the Vaikuntam Vedic Center, as these organizations follow the cultural practices and traditions of South Indians. Similarly, Hindu immigrants from Fiji prefer to visit the Vishnu Temple of the Fiji Sanatan Society of Alberta. Bengali Hindus prefer to attend *Durgāpūjā*, *Kālīpūjā* and other religious events organized by the Edmonton Bengali Association or the Krishti-Bengali Cultural Society.

The practice preferences of different faiths also depend on their deities or spiritual gurus, and accordingly there are specific religious organizations or temples in Edmonton. For example, the Vaikuntam Vedic Center is for the Veṅkaṭeśvara adherents, the temple of the International Swaminarayan Satsang Organization (ISSO) is for the Swami Narayan adherents and the temple of the International Society for Krishna Consciousness (ISKON) is for the Gauḍīya Vaiṣṇava adherents. The followers of Ramakrishna order as well Sathya Sai Baba have their own organizations: the Vedanta Society of Edmonton and the Sri Sathya Sai Baba Centre of Edmonton. The temple of the Bharatiya Cultural Society of Alberta fulfils the needs of the large South Asian Hindu community living in south side of the city, while the HSA is located at the northern corner of the city. Of course, there are overlaps in preferences, and many Hindus do visit different temples or organizations.

The HSA believes in the broader and more inclusive connotation of the term "Hindu" as that which encompasses all different religious traditions originating from the Indian subcontinent. Its Cultural Centre, for example, is the official address of the Jain Society of Alberta. Some of the important *mūrtis* (worship images) in the prayer hall of the Centre are of Mahāvīra, Pārśvanātha and Padmāvatī, saints commonly associated with Jainism. The Hindu Cultural Centre also houses the images of Lord Buddha and Guru Nanak, the key figures of Buddhism and Sikhism respectively. Various Sufi songs and Sikh hymns are also sung at the prayer hall during the *saṅkīrtana* (devotional singing). When he was a volunteer priest, Mr Kalia included celebrations of a number of different religious ceremonies from various parts of India. However, most of the present members of the Society are from the northern and western parts of the Indian subcontinent. Therefore, the HSA predominantly practices the popular North Indian form of Hinduism. The *saṅkīrtana* at the temple is performed primarily in various dialects of Hindustani or Hindi, sometimes in Punjabi and Gujarati and occasionally in Marathi. The priest delivers his discourses most often in Hindi.

Currently, the main activities of the HSA include daily (morning and evening on weekdays and only mornings on weekends) worship, regular Sunday worship and *Prīti Bhojana* (a sacred or divine vegetarian meal given freely to all visitors), observance of various religious ceremonies, celebration of Hindu festivals, and occasional services for the benefit of the community at large.

Early Historical Background

CANADA, BEING A RELATIVELY YOUNG COUNTRY, was a top migration destination that attracted peoples from many parts of the world.[1] The people of the highly populated Indian subcontinent were no exception. Moreover, in the nineteenth and the first half of the twentieth century, both India and Canada were under the same imperial rule that encouraged the subjects of British India to migrate to this new country. However, the racially restrictive immigration regulations of Canada until the 1960s hindered the flow of non-European immigrants to Canada.

The first South Asian settlers in Canada as well as in Alberta were the Sikhs. Before the 1950s, there were only a handful of Sikh farmers living in southern Alberta. In addition to these farmers, a few other Sikhs attended the University of Alberta in the 1920s. In 1947, South Asians in British Columbia were granted suffrage, and other restrictions over South Asian immigration were gradually eased. Most of the South Asian settlers who arrived in the late 1950s were school teachers. They went to small towns and rural areas where there had been a shortage of teachers. According to Canadian census data, 208 South Asians were living in Alberta in 1961.

As a direct result of further changes in the Canadian immigration regulations, comparatively large waves of South Asian immigration began in the 1960s. After Ontario (especially metro Toronto) and British Columbia, Alberta became the prime destination for immigrants of South Asian origin. A very high proportion of these immigrants were Sikhs, but South Asians (commonly referred to as East Indians)

---

1. The information presented in this section is primarily taken from N. Buchignani (1985). 'South Asians in Alberta'. In: *Peoples of Alberta: Portraits of Cultural Diversity*. Saskatoon: Western Producer Prairie Books: 413–36.

Early Historical Background

also became a part of Alberta society in significant numbers during this period. From 1967 on, prospective immigrants were screened primarily on the basis of economic and social criteria; thus, most of the South Asians who migrated during this period were highly skilled. These immigrants came from various ethnic and religious backgrounds but were otherwise experienced tradespersons and professionals from middle-class backgrounds. They were trained in English. Many were teachers, professors, engineers, architects, town planners, economists and skilled servicemen. According to Dr Ram K. Gupta, in 1965 there were approximately two-hundred Indian nationals living in Edmonton, among whom fifteen were professors at the University of Alberta, sixty-five were students, and five or six were schoolteachers.

By 1971, there were approximately 4,400 South Asians in Alberta. Most of them were very recent immigrants to Canada. However, attracted by economic opportunities in Alberta, a small but growing number of immigrants began to arrive from other provinces. They soon formed social networks, based primarily on their various ethnic, religious and national backgrounds. The Hindu Society of Alberta (HSA) was an obvious example of one of these religious networks of association. By the mid-1980s, there were approximately 5,000 Hindus living in Edmonton.

Establishment of the HSA

THE SOUTH ASIAN IMMIGRANTS who initiated the formation of the Hindu Society of Alberta were young and highly skilled. They felt a great urge to establish a community through which they could nurture their religious, cultural, linguistic and ethnic practices, and raise the next generation with their own cultural values. Before the inauguration of the HSA, they held informal gatherings to discuss various religious and spiritual issues and to have a feeling of community life. Much of this early activity centred around the University of Alberta (U of A) and its Indian Students' Association, which was formed in 1964 and is still operating as a students' group today. In its early days, the HSA collaborated with the Indian Students Association of the U of A to organize numerous events. Dr Ram Krishan Gupta, the first General Secretary of the HSA, joined the University of Alberta in 1965 as a professor in the Faculty of Education. During his prior doctoral studies at the University of Minnesota, he participated in the establishment of a Hindu association. He was inspired by this experience, which seems to have been a motivation behind his work to establish the HSA.

Swami Bhashyananda's visit to Edmonton in 1967 was a major inspiration for formalizing the Hindu Society of Alberta. This Hindu monk of the Vivekananda Vedanta Society of Chicago came to the University of Alberta as a visiting lecturer on the life and teachings of Swami Vivekananda. A group of intellectuals held a private session with Swami Bhashyananda, who encouraged them to build an organization to serve Edmonton's growing South Asian community. Dr Sujit Kumar Chakrabartty quotes Swami Bhashyananda:

> Very soon many unskilled laborers of Indian origin will join your community, and they

will bring their traditional beliefs in ritualistic worship and private shrines. Be prepared to welcome them. Build a registered society in accordance to the laws of this land. Under the umbrella of this society, regular programs of prayer, worship and reading of sacred religious texts are to be held. And whenever you need any assistance call us.[1]

Many of the initial members of the HSA were professors, researchers or students of the University of Alberta. These included Dr Ram Krishan Gupta, professor of educational psychology, Dr Ambikeshwar Sharma, professor of mathematics, Dr Mangesh Ganesh Murdeshwar, professor of mathematics, Dr Bhalachandra Vishwanath Paranjape, professor of physics, Dr S. P. Khetarpal, professor of law, Mr Gajanan Pundit, a student in the Faculty of Law, Dr Kamal Nath Jha, a research scientist with the chemistry department, Dr Vinod K. Ratti, a research scientist in the physics department, Mr Jivan Kayande, an undergraduate student in engineering, and Mrs Maya Murdeshwar (Dr Mangesh G. Murdeshwar's wife), a graduate student in the Department of Economics.

The seed of the Society was laid down on November 1, 1967 on the day of Diwali in the basement of Dr Ram Krishan Gupta's house.[2] Thirty-one people attended this event. They contributed one dollar each and became the members of the new Society. Dr Gupta was able to provide the following information regarding attendees of this program: (1) Dr Ram Krishan Gupta and (2) his wife Mrs Indira Gupta; (3) Mr Krishan Chandra Joshee, (4) his wife Mrs Karuna Joshee and (5) his parents Mrs Sumitra Devi Joshee and (6) Mr Arjan Das Joshee; (7) Dr Sujit Kumar Chakrabartty and (8) his wife Mrs Aruna Chakrabartty; (9) Dr P. C. Sood, a

---

1. Sujit Chakrabartty (2015). *Vedanta and Hindu Diaspora in Canada*. Edmonton: Eight Silver Waves – Dolce Veda: 35.
2. Address: 5404 94 B Avenue, Edmonton

post-doctoral fellow from the Department of Physics and (10) his wife; (11) Mr Baldev Raj Abbi and (12) his wife, Mrs Darshan Abbi; (13) Mr Prem Kumar Gupta and (14) his wife; (15) Dr Mangesh Ganesh Murdeshwar and (16) his wife Mrs Maya Murdeshwar; (17) Om Prakash Gupta and (18) his wife, (19); Mr B. B. Prasad and (20) his wife Sita Prasad; (21) and Mr J. N. Sherman, (22) his wife, (23) their daughter and (24) their son. Two other couples and three other individuals completed the group.[3]

In these early days, there was disagreement about including the word "Hindu" in the designation of the Society. Some, such as Dr Saraswati P. Singh, a PhD student and subsequently a professor at the University of Alberta, was in favour of keeping a more generic and inclusive designation. However, Dr Gupta was in favour of retaining the name as a Hindu Society, and this latter designation prevailed.

---

3. Dr Ram Krishan Gupta could not remember all participants' names. There was a Sardar couple; the husband was a student of educational psychology, and his wife was a student in the Department of Political Science. Of the other couple, the husband was a post-doctoral fellow in the Department of Physics.

The HSA: Before Its Cultural Centre

THE HINDU SOCIETY OF ALBERTA had to go a long way before 1981, when it was able to move to its present location. During its early period (1967–1981) the official address of the Society was at the University of Alberta, and many of its activities were carried out on the university campus. This era of the HSA is best understood by dividing into two periods: before and after its official registration with the province of Alberta in 1972.

The HSA: Before Provincial Registration (1967–1972)

The early enthusiasts led by Dr Ram Krishan Gupta formed a five-member committee, comprised of a General Secretary, Treasurer and three additional members. The initial Committee developed a single page constitution. The first executive body was elected in February of 1968. Four out of the five members of this committee were University of Alberta students. They were Mr Gajanan Pundit, Mr Baldev Abbi, Mr Vidyasagar and Mr J. N. Sherman. Dr Gupta was the General Secretary of the Society and remained in that post for three years. In 1971, Dr Raghav Yamdagni, a post-doctoral fellow in the Department of Chemistry became the General Secretary. In 1972, Dr Mangesh Ganesh Murdeshwar assumed the role of General Secretary. However, he resigned during the middle of his term and Mr Uday Bagwe carried his term to completion. In 1973, Dr M. Murdeshwar's wife Mrs Maya Murdeshwar became the General Secretary.

Before it was registered with the provincial government, the Society was called Hindu Society, University of Alberta. In the initial years, many meetings of the HSA were held at the Education Building on the University of Alberta campus.

Sometimes, meetings took place in the Tory Building if there was not enough room in the Education Building. A major activity organized by the HSA at this time was the screening Indian movies, following a tradition established earlier by the Indian Students Organization. Mr Asgar Ali helped to procure the movies, and viewers would purchase tickets for $1 or $1.50. The HSA would view the movies in the Henry Marshall Tory Building of the University of Alberta, usually in room TL-11 in the basement. Mr Uday Bagwe, and later Mr Balvant Gandhi, Mr Shyam Behari and Mr Krishan Kumar Chawla played key roles in planning and hosting these events.

The HSA: After Provincial Registration (1972–1981)

During Mr Uday Bagwe's tenure, the Society was made a registered body under the Societies Act of the Province of Alberta and officially became The Hindu Society of Alberta. On July 12, 1972, the Societies Act application was completed. The signatories for the document were Mr Uday Bagwe, Mr Mangesh Ganesh Murdeshwar, Mrs Sunita Kumar, Mr M. P. Khandekar, and Mr Sujit Kumar Chakrabartty.[1] It was witnessed by Dr Ram K. Gupta. On July 15, 1972 a three-page set of by-laws was created. On August 8, 1972, the application was received by the Office of the Registrar of Companies, Province of Alberta the Certificate of Incorporation was issued, and the Society became a Registered Canadian Charitable Organization, Registration No. 0438051-22-25.

In the fall of 1973, members of the newly formed Society discovered that getting a more permanent space on the University of Alberta campus would not be easy. They thus rented a meeting place close to the campus, at 10436–81 Avenue. However, occasional *pūjā* and other cultural programs still took place on campus. The new location was leased by India

---

1. For details about these individuals see Appendix B, pp. 90 ff.

The HSA: Before Its Cultural Centre

Centre, an organization of people from India that later became known as the Council of India Societies. Government grants facilitated this lease. The HSA and the Maha Ganapathy Society paid rent to the India Centre to use the venue on Sundays. Later on, the Council of India Societies of Edmonton moved to a location close to Calgary Trail. The HSA had some programs at this new location as well. The official address of the Society, however, remained the University of Alberta.

The main activity of early Sunday sessions was reading religious scriptures, especially the *Bhagavadgītā* and its Marathi-language commentary *Jñāneśvarī*. Members would read the original Sanskrit and its Marathi commentary and discuss it in English. The Maratha families, such as Mr and Mrs Murdeshwar would help attendees to understand the Marathi commentary. Later the *Rāmacaritamānasa* was read as well. Readings of the *Gītā* and the *Rāmacaritamānasa* continued on alternating Sundays from 12 noon to 2 pm, with ten to twelve people attending most sessions. Dr Ambikeshwar Sharma took the lead role in reading the scriptures. Early attendees included Mrs Shyam Pundit,[2] Dr Ram Krishan Gupta, his wife Mrs Indira Gupta, Dr Sujit Kumar Chakrabartty, his wife Aruna Chakrabartty, Dr Mangesh Ganesh Murdeshwar and his wife Mrs Maya Murdeshwar, Dr Vembu Gourishankar,[3] Mr Pitambar Lal Avasthi, his wife Mrs Subhadra Avasthi, Mr Siriram Sawhney, his wife Mrs Ramrani Sawheny, Mr Pyarelal Puri, his wife Mrs Maya Puri, and Mr Gajanan Pundit. There was no provision for a lunch to follow, and no worship or other rituals were performed.

However, there was still an unmet need for the performance of religious rituals and rites amongst members of the

---

2. Mrs Pundit, a very enthusiast woman from Lucknow, was Dr Srishti Nigam's mother. Mrs Pundit used to come with Dr Ambikeshwar Sharma. She passed away five years ago in India.

3. A Tamil professor in the Department of Electrical Engineering, University of Alberta. He passed away on May 1, 2017.

Hindu community, especially funerals, marriages and the worship of family deities. Before Mr Sushil Kumar Kalia joined the Society in 1976, Dr Chakrabartty and Dr Murdeshwar would perform some religious ceremonies for individuals on request.

Mr Kalia realized that the HSA could not attract new members only through cultural and academic activities, as the "grassroot community" was more interested in religious ceremonies. Mr Kalia introduced weekly rituals like *pūjā, saṅkīrtana, satsaṅga*, and began leading religious programs. By the end of the 70s, the HSA was already conducting worship program (Bhajans and prayers) along with the reading of the *Rāmāyaṇa* and the *Bhagavadgītā* every Sunday starting at 12:00 noon at the India Centre.

In 1981, the Cultural Centre of the Society became functional. Some HSA members preferred to continue their meetings in the rented space at the India Centre, so regular prayer meetings continued there under the guidance of Dr Ambikeshwar Sharma and Mr Siriram Sawhney. The rent was $75 per month and the Society paid this from the contributions from the people joining these weekly meetings. The Society continued to refer to the India Centre as the "South Side Facility."

The Fabric of the HSA

Objectives

The objectives of the HSA are described in the Societies Act Application 1972. These objectives were modified by resolutions dated December 8, 1974 and April 25, 1993, which are italicized:

1972

(a) To foster the spirit of worship and dedication, and to cultivate the Hindu value of life as suited to modern times.

(b) To diffuse the knowledge of the ethical, spiritual, religious, philosophical and social foundations and practices of Hindu religion and culture.

(c) To promote and conduct activities of cultural, intellectual, social, religious and charitable nature and to undertake all such lawful activities as are deemed conducive to and incidental to the attainment of the above objectives.

(d) To provide for the recreation of the members and to promote and afford opportunity for friendly and social activities.

1974

(a) To foster the spirit of *devotion*, dedication and worship and to cultivate and *propagate* Hindu values *and mores* of life as suited to modern times.

(b) To diffuse knowledge of ethical, spiritual, religious and philosophical foundations and practice of Hindu culture.

(c) To provide for the recreation of *the public at large through yoga, meditation, music, dancing, and such other* activities *as are related to Hindu heritage.*

(d) To promote and afford opportunities for social and multicultural activities.

(e) To promote respect and understanding between Hindus and *various ethno-cultural groups of Canada.*

(f) To promote respect and understanding between Hindus and others.

(e) To provide a meeting place for the consideration and discussion of questions effecting the interests of the community.

(f) *To help people in emergency.*

(g) *To develop and maintain one or more religious and cultural centers.*

(g) To build or buy a cultural center. [1993]

(h) To promote, conduct, and *carry on* activities of cultural, intellectual, social, religious, and charitable nature and undertake all such lawful activities as are deemed conducive to and incidental to the attainment and realization of the above objectives.

Official Address

The first official address of the HSA was on the University of Alberta campus:[1]

>Hindu Society of Alberta
>The University of Alberta
>P.O. Box A 363
>Edmonton T6G 2E8.

The HSA used the university address for their official correspondence until 1984. One official document dated August 20, 1982 mentions the address of the Hindu Cultural Centre (14225–133 Avenue) along with the official address of the HSA as the University of Alberta. By a notice dated August 31, 1984 the address of the HSA was officially changed to

---

1. A letter was sent to the Registrar of Companies, Govt. of the Province of Alberta mentioning the official address of the Society.

Hindu Cultural Centre
14225–133 Avenue,
Edmonton,
Alberta.

By-laws

The structure and the rules of the Society are described in its by-laws. At the time of the establishment of the Society in 1967, it had a one-page constitution. The first by-laws were created with the provincial registration of the Society in 1972. Over time, the by-laws have been modified several times. The by-laws were amended on December 11, 1974, May 16, 1983, April 25, 1993, April 5, 2002, July 25, 2012, and most recently on February 14, 2016.

Administration

The HSA has been run by an elected body since its inception. From 1967 to 1972, the Society was managed by a five-member committee. After the provincial registration in August 1972, the Executive Committee remained more or less the same. It consisted of the General Secretary with three other elected members: the Joint Secretary, the Treasurer and the Auditor. The fiscal and operational year of the society ran from October 1 of one year to September 30 of the following year.

The by-laws of the HSA revised on December 11, 1974 increased the Executive of the HSA from five to six members, including: (i) President (ii) Vice President (Programs) (iii) Vice President (Cultural Centre) (iv) Secretary (v) Secretary-Treasurer (Programs) and (vi) Secretary-Treasurer (Cultural Centre). The revised bylaws reflected the organisation's growing size and complexity. The fiscal and operational year was changed to the first day of January to the last day of December each year. The by-laws fleshed out the HSA's original constitution. The by-laws divided the HSA into two constituents: (i) a General Body, and (ii) Donors and Patrons. The general body consisted of regular members of the HSA. Those who donated at least $100 in a year for the purpose of building the planned Cultural Centre were deemed Donors during that year. Patrons were those who donated or pledged to donate a minimum of $500 within any five-year period. Patron was a lifetime designation for those who honoured their commitment.

In the 1974 amendments, the authority of the HSA was established with a fifteen-member Board of Directors of the Society. The Board, in accordance with the twofold division of the Society, was also divided into two parts: (i) a seven-member Program Committee and (ii) an eight-member Cultural Centre Committee. The seven members of the Program Committee were elected from the General Body. One of these seven persons was elected as Vice President (Programs) and one as Secretary–Treasurer (Programs).

The eight members of the Cultural Center were elected by patron and donor members from amongst themselves. One of the seven persons was elected as Vice President (Cultural Centre) and one as Secretary-Treasurer (Cultural Centre). A provisional committee of the Cultural Centre had already been established by 1974. Dr Ram Krishan Gupta was the provisional Vice President of the Cultural Centre committee. The annual elections for the two constituencies were proposed to be held at the Annual General Body Meeting on or shortly before December 10th. The elected members took charge on January 1st and served until the end of the year.

In further amendments of the by-laws in 1993, the fiscal year of the society was altered to commence on the first day of April and end on the last day of March in the following year. The operational year of the society commenced on the fifteenth day of May and ended on the fourteenth day of May in the following year. The new by-laws amended the management of the Society as well. The managing body was divided into two elected bodies: (a) The Executive Committee and (b) The Board of Directors. The Executive Committee consisted six members as before. But there remained only one Treasurer and a new post of the immediate past president was introduced. The Board consisted 15 members as before, but its configuration changed to that of five elected members of the Executive Committee, plus ten other elected members of whom at least three are life members.

In amendments to the by-laws in 2012, the post of the third Vice-President for Public Relations and Communications was included. In further amendments in 2016, the operational year was removed and members were able to run only for one office and not multiple positions. Also, the requirement of a minimum of three life members was removed.

Membership

The membership rules of the HSA were also modified from time to time over the years. In the 1972 by-laws, there were three categories of members: regular, associate and junior. These categories were elaborated in the 1974 by-laws. Regular members were described as persons or families who applied for membership to the HSA and paid prescribed dues. Regular members had the right to vote at any meeting, to hold any office, to sign requisitions for special meetings, and to sign no-confidence motions. Associate members were persons or families who applied for membership to the HSA and paid the prescribed dues. Dues for associate memberships were lower than those for regular membership, but associate members did not have the right to give or receive votes, or to receive notices from the General Body meetings of the HSA. Junior members were under the age of eighteen and their parents were members of the Society.

Initially, obtaining membership in the Society was comparatively difficult. Any adult could apply for membership by paying the membership fee, but his/her membership had to be approved through a favourable vote passed by a majority of the Executive. Pending such a vote, the person was regarded as a provisional member. If the provisional member was not accepted, his/her payment was refunded in full. The membership fee was determined by the Executive Committee.

In the late seventies, some non-Hindu people also became members of the Society. Mr and Mrs Grossman, a Jewish couple, joined as members, and there were some Sikh members by this time as well. A by-law amended in 1983 made the process of obtaining membership much easier. The by-law states:

> Any person who accepts the objectives of the Society shall be eligible to become a member.

This by-law added three more categories of membership. These are described as follows:

Honorary Life Members An individual who has given meritorious and extraordinary service to the Society, in recognition of which the Board unanimously decides to invite him/her to Honorary Life Membership.

Life Members Any person or agency who has donated to the Society $500 or more by June 31, 1983, or who does so during any three successive years, starting August 1983, shall have one vote. Starting January 1, 1993, the life membership fee is $500 to be paid within one calendar year. Donations can be made by a person for spouses or children.

Donors Any person or agency who has donated at least $200 to the Society, becomes a donor for one year, starting the date of the donation, and shall have one vote.

The other categories of regular members, associate members and junior members remained the same.

This by-law amendment also granted membership to associations or societies. The rule is described as follows: "Any incorporated organization can become member of the Society by paying annual dues set by the Board. The president or a delegate of the joining organization will have voting rights in the annual elections of the Society."

The Fabric of the HSA

Since by-law amendments in 2012, the HSA has recognized four types of membership: (1) Honorary Life Members (2) Life Members (3) Regular Members and (4) Membership to Association/Society.

Fundraising

During the early days of the HSA, funding reflected the small and less formal nature of the fledgling organization. Funds were raised mainly from donations and screening Hindi movies. The price of the tickets for these screenings was $1 or $1.50 per person. The largest donation to the Society during the first six years was $60 from the late Dr Bhattacharya.

In 1972, the HSA became a Registered Canadian Charitable Organization, which created more opportunities for formal fundraising. Contributions to the HSA were now tax-deductible. After the establishment of the temple at the HCC, many affluent Hindu families who live in and around Edmonton started coming to the temple. Their donations further strengthened the financial position of the Society.

In the early 1980s, the HSA was running deficits. The society was repaying a debt to the Bank of British Columbia. The Hindu Cultural Centre had been expanded, and there were financial challenges to keeping up the facility and sustaining its programs. Expansion and renovation had not left enough funds for operating expenses and wages. In order to meet these challenges, and to function without any hardship, the Board had to come together to organize many special *pūjās* to raise funds, with the creative guidance of the priest.

In 1981, Mr K. C. Joshee[2], who eventually became the Chair of the Alberta Gaming Commission, introduced to the Society the idea of volunteering with bingos as a potentially significant revenue source for the HSA. Casinos were introduced for raising funds during the mid-80s and became an additional source of fundraising. Mr Kayande, Mr Khullar,

---

2. For further details about Mr Joshee, please see Appendix B, p. 91.

and Mr Aggrawal became guarantors for the HSA when it began taking part in casinos for fund-raising. Mr K. C. Joshee, Mr Jivan Kayande, Mr Ramesh Chander Khullar, Mr Ashwini Bhasin, Mr Krishan Kumar Chawla, Mr Pitambar Lal Avasthi and Mr Ramesh Aggrawal contributed to the management of volunteers. Mr Kayande's and Mr Khullar's families also regularly volunteered for the bingos and casinos themselves. Presently, the Society volunteers in casinos every two years.

The Society has also received government grants, and initially was quite dependent upon them. The government provided grants matching funds that the Society was able to raise from other sources on a dollar-to-dollar basis. Mr Krishan Chandra Joshee played an important role in securing many such grants in the HSA's early years. However, the government gradually reduced its direct funding of societies and community organizations, which required the HSA to rely more on other sources of funding including casinos.

Youth Involvement

Children and youth have always made active contributions to the HSA. The 1972 by-laws recognized junior members as one of the three types of members. When parents became members, their unmarried children under age 18 became automatically junior members. Junior members did not have voting rights. The 2012 by-laws, however, removed the junior member category, and youth are now included in other categories of members. Youths volunteer in singing Bhajans and playing instruments. They write pieces in the annual *Patrika* magazine, help in organizing rituals and programmes, assist in the kitchen and help to serve food. The HSA organizes worship of Goddess Sarasvatī twice in a year exclusively for school children. Children perform in Janmāṣṭamī and in Makara Saṅkrānti (Lohri). The HSA organizes various weekly activities exclusively for its youth members.

The Hindu Cultural Centre

IN 1971, EDGAR PETER LOUGHEED became the tenth Premier of Alberta. He established the Alberta Heritage Fund in 1976. During his tenure, various ethnocultural groups were supported. A political climate of liberalism and multiculturalism fostered the creation of different religious and cultural societies. This support and welcoming environment helped the Society to take steps toward building the Hindu Cultural Centre on the north side of Edmonton.

Background and Planning

In 1972, the Society appointed a Building Committee, with Dr Murdeshwar as Chairman, to explore the possibility of building or acquiring a physical facility for the Society. Then, Dr Ram K. Gupta became the Chairman. The other members of the Building Committee were Mr Satish Rao, Mr Lok Sharma and Mr Uttam Chandani.

In the 1974 by-laws, the Hindu Cultural Centre was proposed as an operating centre for the HSA. The Centre was to be built on land in the City of Edmonton or its vicinity that would be purchased, leased or otherwise acquired. The Cultural Centre of the HSA was proposed to be open for everyone: The 1974 by-laws recommended,

> The use of the Center shall be guided by the philosophy of sharing. It will, therefore, be available to all, irrespective of color, creed, religion, or place of origin.

The City of Edmonton leased 1.18 acres of land beside St. Albert Trail to multicultural communities for the establishment of gathering places. Societies registered these as cultural rather than religious centres, again with the intent of welcoming outsiders and building bridges of cultural understanding.

On this land, which was named Peter Lougheed Multicultural Village in 1985, four cultural centres were built: (1) the Hindu Cultural Center, (2) Siri Guru Nanak Sikh Gurdwara (3) the Italian Cultural Centre and (4) the Dutch Canadian Centre. Mr B. B. Prasad helped the Society to obtain the land lease from the City of Edmonton. The lease was signed in 1974 by Edmonton's mayor, Dr Ivor Dent, on the stage of Jubilee Auditorium, when Padmini performed. The initial lease was for twenty years (June 1, 1974 to May 31, 1994). The rental agreement was as follows:

- One percent of the assessed value of the land payable each year in advance. The assessed value shall be determined by the City Assessor at the time when this agreement is executed; and revised every five (5) years thereafter by the City Assessor;
- In addition to the foregoing, the Lessee shall pay as rent a sum equal to yearly taxes, also determined by the City Assessor from year to year, plus all local improvement and frontage charges.

The lease agreement was signed by Dr Kamal Nath Jha and Dr Ram Krishna Gupta.

The *Bhūmi-pūjana* (sod-turning ceremony) for the HSA building took place on August 7, 1976 under the guidance of Swami Nihshreyasananda (see illustration on p. 26). Dr Kamal Nath Jha, then president of the Society, became the formal sponsor of this ritual (Sanskrit *yajamāna*). The main program was held at the Dutch Cultural Center. The plaque outside the building states:

> This plaque gratefully acknowledges the commitment & dedication of the members of the Hindu Society of Alberta who initiated the Hindu Cultural Centre project in 1976. Blessed by Swami Nihshreyasananda at the sod-turning ceremony performed by Hon. Horst A. Schmid, Minister of Culture, Government of the Province of Alberta on August 7, 1976.

In his statement on the occasion of the Foundation Stone Ceremony, Dr Ram Krishan Gupta announced that the Society had already raised about $75,000 towards a more than $300,000 estimated construction cost. Mr Krishan Chandra Joshee was instrumental in securing further financial support.

Hindu Cultural Centre (HCC) Building Timeline

1972: The board of the Hindu Society of Alberta (HSA) appoints a building committee

1976, August 7: *Bhūmi-pūjana* (sod turning) takes place for phase I.

1979: Construction (phase 1) of HCC begins.

1984, June 12: *Bhūmi-pūjana* performed for the phase II extension.

1984, June 21: Foundation stone for the phase II proposed extension was laid.

1984, September 15: The members of the HSA dedicate the Hindu Cultural Centre to the citizens of Edmonton.

1989: The HSA purchases land and takes $56,000 mortgage from the Canadian Imperial Bank of Commerce.

1991: Phase II extension gets completed with the extended prayer hall. 3,300 sq. ft. added to the main floor and similar area added to the basement.

1993, September 19: A motion is made to apply for permit for the phase III extension.

1994, January: After the plan is approved a storage space added beside the older stage where Navagraha shrine is presently located, a two-story residence was added to provide accommodation for priest.

2004–2008: Phase IV expansion takes place which was divided in two projects.

2004–2005: Phase IV first project completed- larger facility for toilets was built upstairs, library was shifted to the boardroom, a small area from the front of the prayer

Alberta Cultural Minister Horst Schmid turns sod for the new Hindu Cultural Centre. *Edmonton Journal*, 7 August 2013.

hall was taken for keeping the shoe racks and the coat racks.

2005–2006: Phase IV second project completed – Swami Vivekananda Hall was built expanding beyond the priest quarter, basement under this hall was dug and the kitchen was shifted there, Basement was extended, and the two unconnected basements were connected to create a dining hall.

2006–2008: Finishing completed for phase IV first and second project.

Phase 1

The project of building the HCC began in 1979, five years after the feasibility and concept study initiated in 1974. Due to uncertain cash-flow and funding, the project was planned and budgeted for development in phases.

To kick-start the project, the Society applied to the Provincial Government for a grant. Sardar Buta Singh, who was constructing the Sikh Cultural Centre beside the HCC, was a great source of information and support in helping the Society to get financial supports. Both Indian cultural centres, the Hindu and the Sikh, enjoyed a cooperative relationship. On May 11, 1979, the Society received a grant of $147,490 from the Provincial Government for the construction of the HCC. The capital construction fund was operated by the Society on a 50:50 share basis between the Society's fund-raising activities and the Province of Alberta grant given in three instalments.

Mr K. K. Sanon oversaw the construction, which began in 1979 using blueprints prepared by the architect Satish Rao who later moved to Ottawa, and Mr Lok Sharma. Land preparation and construction of the basic shell of the building were completed in the summer of 1981 at a cost of $283,000. Then, exterior painting, interior framing, plumbing, heating, electrical wiring, were finished. The total expenditure for this first phase was approximately $600,000. The expense was covered with the funds received from the members' donation and the Provincial Government grants.

When it first opened, the HCC constituted of (1) a Hindu temple (200 sq. ft.), and a community hall, library-cum-class room and kitchen (6,200 sq. ft.). The original space also provided for the prayer hall to be used on weekdays as a day-care and kindergarten. Later, this service was discontinued. On July 19, 1981, the *Gāyatrī Havana* ritual was performed at the cultural centre. The *Havana* ritual was performed by Mr Sushil Kalia with the assistance of Dr Sujit Chakrabartty. With the phase I completion more members started using the space which increase the revenue through donations.

After completion of the construction of the first phase, Sadguru Sant Keshavdas Jee performed the *Bhūmi-pūjā* for the proposed extension of the HCC on June 12, 1984. The foundation stone of the HCC extension for phase II was laid by Swami Bhashyananda from Vedanta Society, Chicago on June 21, 1984. The formal inauguration of the HCC took place on September 15, 1984, with over 100 attendees. Brahmacharini Pavitra, a nun and a member of the Chinmaya mission, blessed the official opening. Marking the occasion, the plaque outside the building states:

> On this day, the 15th of September, 1984, the members of the Hindu Society of Alberta dedicated the Hindu Cultural Centre to the citizens of Edmonton, witnessed by Hon. Horst A. Schmid, Minister of International Trade, Govt. of Alberta, Hon. Mary J. Le Messurier, Minister of Culture, Govt. of Alberta, and His Worship Laurence Decore, Mayor, The City of Edmonton.

On this occasion, the Society received a government grant of $4,000.

Purchase of Land from the City of Edmonton

Gradually, the Italian Cultural Society and the Dutch Canadian Club began using their buildings for commercial purposes, holding weddings, banquets and other private social events. The Hindu Cultural Centre and the Sikh Society of Alberta continued to use their premises mainly for religious purposes. Hotel owners and some other businesses complained to the City that these cultural centers have an unfair advantage as they did not pay any taxes or paid any rent were running commercial activity. The City of Edmonton consequently raised lease/tax assessments in 1982 for all four organizations. In 1986, the Society owed approximately $50,000 in property taxes to the City of Edmonton.

The cultural centres were agitated by this decision and organized to oppose it. The Edmonton Cultural Caucus was formed with the objective to have these taxes waived. The Caucus represented societies of the Hindus, Sikhs, Jews and several others. Mr K. C. Joshee served as Vice-Chairman. The Caucus met with the City to seek a fair assessment. Mayor Lawrence Decore was very sympathetic to the plight of the cultural centres. The Minister of Municipal Affairs, Mr J. Koziak indicated that the issue could be resolved amicably.

The Minister of Culture, Mr D. Anderson tried to negotiate with the City of Edmonton on a formula to share taxes, but these efforts were turned down by City Council. The Cultural Centres tried in court to not to have to pay taxes. In 1989 the court gave a decision in favour of The City. By this time the HSA had saved $89,000 in back taxes. At this time the City of Edmonton offered each of the centres to buy their own land at market value. The HSA had money saved for the back taxes but did not have any funds to purchase the land. During President JIvan Kayande's tenure in 1989–1990 the HSA borrowed $56,000 for mortgage from the Canadian Imperial Bank of Commerce (CIBC). The balance of the mortgage was paid off when Jivan Kayande became president during 1997–1998.

Phase 2

The foundation stone for phase II expansion was laid on June 21, 1984 and in 1991, during the tenure of Balvant Gandhi, the prayer hall was extended up to its current size and the basement underneath the addition was built. Approximately 3300 sq. ft. on the main floor and an equal area in the basement were added. The Society received a grant of $143,000 for this project. Mr Satish Rao, a member of the HSA helped to find contractors, as he himself was an architect. Dr Ram Gupta also helped through his contacts. A funding shortfall of $30,000 was covered by a loan from Mr Ramesh Aggarwal and his business partner. In the meantime, the Society applied for a grant for the needed funds. MLA Ken Kowalski presented a cheque for a $30,000 grant when he attended the opening ceremony for the expansion. With these funds, the HSA repaid the loan to Mr Aggarwal and his partner.

Phase 3

In a board meeting held on September 19, 1993, Mr Naresh Sharma proposed that "the Hindu Society of Alberta should apply for the permit for the extension of the Hindu Cultural Centre." This was seconded by Mr Amar Bhasin, and all other members were in favour. Additional changes to the Hindu Cultural Centre took place after a plan was approved in January 1994. At this time, Mrs Poonam Mehra was President of the HSA. For this expansion, a storage area was built beside the older stage where the Navagraha deities are presently located. A two-story addition was added to provide a residence for the priest. Alberta Hindi Parishad donated $5,000 for the construction. Mr Rajiv Ranjan was the president of the Alberta Hindi Parishad during this construction.

Phase 4

The final expansion of the HCC took place during the tenures of Mr Preetam Sharma and Mr Rajiv Ranjan (2004–2008) and their boards. Dr R. L. Singh was the project manager. The money for the expansion came through fund-raising with the help of devotees, businesses, volunteers and government grants. The Society applied for government grants through the CIP (Community Initiative Program), and the following year through the CFEP (Community Facility Enhancement Program). The expansion project was divided into two separate projects in order to utilize these funds over two years. The Hindu Society of Alberta received $250,000 in total. As per the requirement of these grants the HSA raised a matching amount.

In the first project (2004–2005), toilets were built in the room adjacent to the main entrance, which had been the library. The library was shifted to the boardroom, next to the office. Prior to this build, the HCC already had two toilets, a small one adjacent to the office room, which is presently

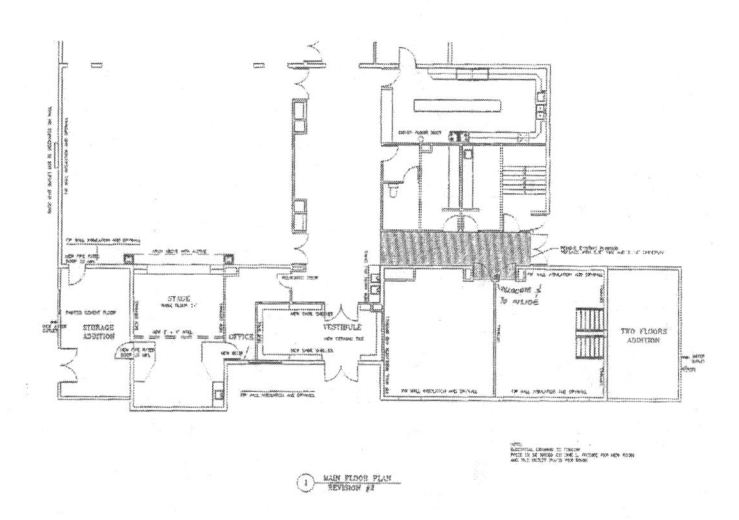

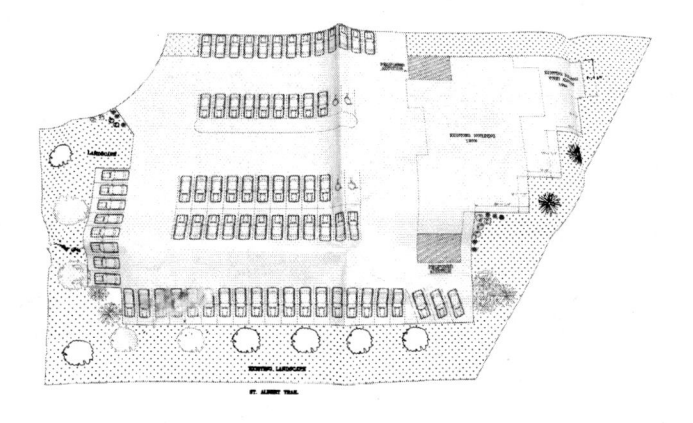

Construction blueprints for Phase 3.

exclusively for the physically challenged people, and a larger one in the basement under the office and boardroom area. However, most people were not using the toilet in the basement, leading to long queues for the smaller main floor toilet. Board members thus decided to build a larger facility on the main floor. As part of the same project, a small area from the front part of the prayer hall was reconfigured. The pedestal of statues was moved to the opposite side of the hall to accommodate shoe and coat racks. This was a necessary step as the number of members had increased significantly by this time.

The second project (2005–2006) extended the basement to create a dining hall. Prior to this project, food had been served right outside of the prayer hall and people would eat in the prayer hall sitting on the floor. As the population was aging, the Committee felt the need to build a dining hall with tables and chairs. They also wanted to keep the prayer hall tidy and clean. A large dining hall and a kitchen were thus built in the basement, and approximately 400 chairs and 40 tables were purchased for the dining hall. Following the construction and addition of the new space much of finishing was completed during Rajiv Ranjan's tenure (2006–2008).

The second project also included building Swami Vivekananda Hall, expanding the HCC beyond the priest's quarters. The addition included a new basement area, to which the kitchen was moved. Basement excavation and renovations joined two areas of the basement under the prayer hall that had not been connected. The stair to the basement going down from the prayer hall was widened. An elevator was installed for seniors and persons with disabilities, with the funds contributed by Alta Window Manufacturing. The other major sponsor of the elevator was the Kalra Family. The kitchen was fully finished with new cabinets and an exhaust canopy.

The first *Jīrṇoddhāra* ceremony (purifying the murtis of gods and goddesses after the renovations) took place June 22–24, 2007. Many members and devotees attended this special celebration. Alberta Government ministers Dave Hancock and Gene Zwozdesky, and Mayor Stephen Mandel attended this event. The Society was presented with $5,000 from Alberta's Wild Rose Foundation to refurbish carpets, tables, chairs and other interior fixtures in the present library, and to complete the interior of the Swami Vivekanand Hall. Interior finishing, including the Swami Vivekanand Hall and the Navagraha deities was completed during the tenure of President Rajeshwar Singh (2008–2010) and his board.

Between 2011–2012 President Renu Narang and the board finished setting up the picture gallery in the Swami Vivekanand Hall and people began to use this space for yoga and other programs. The Sai Baba *mūrti* (statue) and Jalārām Bāpā *mūrti* were installed at this time as well.

Further renovations to the HCC occurred during Mr Amar Bhasin's tenure as President and his board (2013–2015). The renovation included, major repairs of the domes (*śikhara*) and the roof. The building was refurbished with new doors, new carpets, new flooring, window awnings, new shoe racks and new lights. Concrete work around the HCC was completed and Bālāji *mūrtis* were installed. After this renovation another *Jīrṇoddhāra* ceremony took place on September 5–7, 2014.

Unexpected additional repairs during this renovation created a shortfall of funds for completing the outside window finishing and the addition of a mural on the north-facing exterior wall. Under the leadership of Mr Sushil Kalia and with the help of devotees, $9,000 was raised to complete the project.

President Gunjan Sharma (2015–2016) and her board completed the roof repairs and had the music system installed.

Installation of *Mūrtis* (Statues and Images)

Over the years, many Society members have contributed to the installation of religious statues and images (Sanskrit *mūrti*).[1] Today, the collection represents a broad spectrum of Hindu religious practices. The temple in the HCC was originally a smaller meditation/prayer hall. The hall extended from the main entrance up to the point where, today, there are two pillars.

Praṇava and Gāyatrī Cakra

On the stage of the prayer hall is a symbol of Praṇava (ॐ) and the Gāyatrī Cakra (see figure on p. 35). These were designed by Mr Kalia and were installed on a pedestal during a three-day long installation ritual (Sanskrit *sthāpanā*) held on May 7–9, 1982. Presently, the Praṇava is on the wall inside the main sanctum, above the Śivaliṅga. The Gāyatrī Cakra is on the western wall of the prayer hall.

Bālamukunda

Mr Balvant Gandhi donated a small *mūrti* of Bālakṛṣṇa or Gopāla which was placed in front of the Gāyatrī Cakra and the Praṇava. The marble Bālagopāla was given to devotees.

Pañcadevatā

On May 21, 1983, the *mūrti*s of five deities, Mahāgaṇapati, Śiva, Devī, Viṣṇu and Sūryanārāyaṇa, were installed in the prayer hall through an installation ritual (Sanskrit *prāṇapratiṣṭhā*). The temple of the HCC was then called Pañcāyatana (the House of the Five Deities). The bronze deities were made in Poompuhar (ancient Kaveripoompattinam) in Tamil Nadu. A magazine entitled *Panch Devta Pran Pratishtha Souvenir* was published to mark the occasion. The Society received blessings from Sringeri Guru Maharaj, Swami Satyamitranand Jee, Rishi Keshvanand Jee, Swami Bhashyananda Jee (Chicago) and Divine Mother of Rajarajeshwari Peetham. The major donors for this installation were: Ms Durga Devi from Punjab, Dr Ram Krishan

---

1. Information about donors is taken from the memorial plaques placed on the outer wall of the temple hall, or from printed souvenirs or provided by Mr Sushil Kumar Kalia.

The Hindu Cultural Centre

Praṇava, Gāyatrī Cakra and Pañcadevatā.

Gupta, Mr Gulshan Sawhney, Mr Pran Sawhney, Mr Arvind Sawhney, Dr S. P. Singh, Mr Braj Prasad, Dr Krishan Katyal, Mr Ramesh Agarwal, Mr Uday Bagwe, Mr Bishambar Trikha, Dr Rameshwar Sharma, Mrs Gayatri Sharma, Mrs Nirmal Sanon and Mr Kewal Sanon.

Mahāvīra

On March 19, 1989, the *mūrti* of Mahāvīra was installed in the temple with proper religious ceremonies conducted by Mr Sushil Kumar Kalia and assisted by Jasvant Mehta and Mahendra Mehta. Mr Sheel Chand and Sudha Rani Jain from Dewas, Madhya Pradesh donated the murtis. The Katyal family (Suresh, Usha, Sachin, Shaunik and Millie) donated towards the cost of the marble work. Many other donors contributed to this installation as well.

Śiva-liṅga

The Śiva-liṅga was installed on August 25, 1991. The donors were Mr Ramesh Aggarwal and his family and Mr Raj Bagga and his family.

Rādhā-Kṛṣṇa and Rāma-Sītā-Lakṣmaṇa-Hanumān

The *mūrti*s of Rādhā and Kṛṣṇa were installed on August 21, 1992, and the *mūrti*s of Rāma, Sītā, Lakṣmaṇa and Hanumān were installed on May 30, 1993. The Sanon family was the principal donor. The Khullar family, Mrs Usha Kapur and her family as well as the Bhasin family contributed.

Durgā Ambā

The *mūrti* of Goddess Durgā (Sherawali) was installed on October 9, 1994. Mrs Motia Bhasin undertook the initiative to fund this installation. Other major donors were Mrs Usha Kapur, Mr Krishan Katyal, Mrs Lata Katyal, Mr Sudhir Sahi, Mrs Neelam Sahi, Mrs Viran Anand, Mr Amar Bhasin, Mrs Monica Bhasin, Mr Arvind Sawhney, Mrs Usha Sawhney, Mr Ram Sharma, Mrs Kamlesh Sharma, Mr Sushil Kalia,

The Hindu Cultural Centre

Mrs Kamala Kalia, Mr Braj Prasad, Mrs Sita Prasad, Mr Pran Sawhney, Mrs Nisha Sawhney, Mr Ramesh Khullar, Mrs Kamlesh Khullar, Mr Prabhu Dayal Sarhadi, Mrs Sarla Sarhadi, Mrs Jiwan Jyoti, Mr Shiv Jyoti, Mr Vijay Sawhney, Mrs Veena Sawhney, Mr Ramesh Aggarwal and Mr Vijay Aggarwal.

Ṛṣabhadeva and Pārśvanātha

The *mūrtis* of these two Jain Tīrthaṅkaras were installed on April 7, 1996. The donors were Mr Pradeep Mehta, Mrs Meena Mehta, Mr Jinendra Shah and Mrs Savita Shah.

Navagraha

In 2009, the images of the Navagrahas (Nine Celestial Bodies) were installed in the north end of the prayer hall where the old shrine was. The *prāṇapratiṣṭhā* ceremony was held on June 22–24, 2009. The ceremony was well attended. The HSA received donations from the following societies for the Navagraha installation ceremony and the Mātā Kī Caukī celebration: Alberta Hindi Parishad, the Jhankar Society for Dance and Music, the Manav Seva Association, the Edmonton Raga-Mala Music Society, the Society of Friends of Nepal, the Vedanta Society of Edmonton and the Council of India Society of Edmonton. With the help of Mr Sushil Kalia and other devotees a total of $69,000 was raised for the Navagraha installation ceremony. A panel of Daśāvatāra (Ten Incarnations of Lord Viṣṇu) was placed above the Navagraha sanctum.

Swami Vivekananda Hall Picture Gallery Opening

The picture gallery in the Swami Vivekananda Hall was created on the occasion of the 148th birth anniversary celebration of Swami Vivekananda in 2011. The celebration was held on January 23, 2011. The event was attended by Mr Amarjit Sohi, Mr Naresh Bhardwaj and other dignitaries and devotees. Rajiv Ranjan, then president of the Vedanta society of Edmonton read the messages from Swami Kripamayananda and Swami Bhaskarananda. The HSA was the main organizer and the Vedanta Society of Edmonton helped. The gallery consists of various historical images of Swami Vivekananda and a symbolic figure of Gaṇeśa representing the five elements or the Pañcamahābhūta (earth, water, fire, wind and sky). Mr Sushil Kumar Kalia designed the gallery. The artisans of the design, construction and installation were Mr Arvind Kapur and Mr Rishi Kapur.

Veṅkaṭeśvara with Śrīdevī or Padmāvatī, Bhūdevī and Garuḍa

These *mūrti*s were installed on September 7, 2014, on the occasion of the *prāṇapratiṣṭhā* ceremony. A *Kīrtimukha* and a *Saṭhāri* (a blessing crown) were also installed.

The donors were: Indra Vishnu and family, Paras Technical Services, Mr and Mrs Kanak Prasad Chamarty and family, Dharma Sanassy, Swabbz, Saras and Bijendra Singh, Srinivas Seturaman, Atul Seth, At IT Solution, Ruchika and Pankaj Chopra, Krishna Murthi, Savitri Chandrika Narayan, Kamla and Sushil Kalia, Bindya Deepak Chaitanya, Anjana Marwaha, Varun Grover, Dilip Dasmohapatra, Renu Sharma, Sarla Sharma, Monica and Amar Bhasin, Gulshan Bhutani, Sumedh Renu BhardwajRajni Kalra, Janak Kalra, and Dilip Deshpande. A total of $44,786 was raised for this project.

Nṛtya-Gaṇapati Pañcāyatana Mural

A mural with Dancing Gaṇeśa at the centre and Viṣṇu, Śiva, Devī and Sūrya on four corners, designed by Mr Sushil Kumar Kalia, was installed on the north-facing outside wall of the HCC building on November 22, 2015 during President Mrs Gunjan Sharma's tenure. The mural was unveiled by David Eggen, Minister of Education and Minister of Culture and Tourism.

Other Images

A *mūrti* of Gopāla resides inside the main sanctum. The main donation for this *mūrti* came from Mrs Usha Kapoor, mother of Mr Arvind Kapoor. Close to the main sanctum there are *mūrti*s of Dancing Gaṇeśa, Lord Buddha, (the donation for the stone Buddha came from Mr Sushil Kalia and Mrs Kamala Kalia), Goddess Padmāvatī, and Hanumān. The *mūrti*s of Jalārām Bāpā and Shirdi Sāi Baba on either side of the Navagraha shrine were installed in 2012. Rajan and Dolly Ahluwalia were the principal sponsors of the Sai Baba *mūrti*. Mr Gopal Chawda and family and Mrs Santa Somaiya donated the *mūrti* of Jalārām Bāpā.

The prayer hall also houses numerous photographs. Beside Shirdi Sāi Baba's, *mūrti*, there is a painting of Goddess Lakṣmī with Sarasvatī and Gaṇeśa. The shrine of the Navagraha consists of *mūrti*s as well as paintings of the Navagrahas. At the back of the Navagraha shrine, there is a photo of Lord Naṭarāja. Beside Jalārām Bāpā's *mūrti* there is a painting of Lord Nārāyaṇa. The western wall of the prayer hall is adorned by photographs of Sathya Sai Baba, Lord Gaṇeśa, Hanumān and three Yantras. The eastern wall displays photographs of Guru Nānak, Rādhā and Kṛṣṇa, Rāma with Sītā, Lakṣmaṇa and Hanumān, Goddess Sarasvatī, and another three Yantras. At the back of the main sanctum, there are photographs of Lord Śiva, Hanumān, Goddess Vaiṣṇo Devī/Durgā and Śatruñjaya Tīrtha (Palitana Jain temples of Shatrunjay Hill, Gujarat). The photographs of Guru Nānak Dev and Sathya Sāi Baba were placed on June 19, 1988 in a portrait inauguration ceremony.

The Priest

THE ORIGINAL INTENTION of the Hindu Society of Alberta was to create a community space. Initially, there was no temple and no priest. Occasionally, Dr Sujit Kumar Chakrabartty and Dr Mangesh Ganesh Murdeshwar would perform some rituals on personal request. Regular worship and rituals were introduced in 1976 by Mr Sushil Kumar Kalia, who is now considered the Honorary Priest of the HSA.[1]

After the establishment of the HCC and the temple hall inside it, attendance increased significantly. There was now a need for regular weekly worship. Mr Kalia's involvement and service to the temple had always been voluntary. In 1986, Committee members decided to appoint a permanent priest. The position was advertised both publicly and through personal communications. On August 14, 1987, the HSA issued an appointment letter to Shri Mahant R. D. Sharma of Shri Durga Sankirtan Mandal of Pritam Pura, Delhi. For unknown reasons the correspondence failed, and the Committee had to continue its search. Mr Ramesh Aggarwal, a member of the HSA, asked his guru Rishi Keshavanand Maharaj of Haridwar to suggest some additional eligible applicants. Three persons applied from Rishi Keshavanand Maharaj's Rishi Sanskrit Mahavidyalay. One of them, Acharya Shiv Shankar Dwivedi from Nirdhan Niketan Ashram of Haridwar, was selected. On November 23, 1988, the Society sent an appointment letter to him. He arrived in Edmonton on September 11, 1989 and was appointed as the priest of the temple of the Hindu Cultural Centre.

Acharya Dwivedi is a philanthropist who is well-versed in Hindu scriptures.[2] He studied Sanskrit literature at Sampurnanand Sanskrit University, Varanasi. He has Ph.D. and

---

1. See Appendix B, p. 86, for further details about Mr Kalia.
2. See Appendix B, p. 87, for further details about Acharya Dwivedi.

The Priest

is a Gold Medalist in Sanskrit. He was a disciple of Rishi Keshavanand Maharaj of Haridwar. A documentary of Acharya Dwivedi's life called "The Three Lives of Panditji" was directed by Robert Chelmick, an award-winning television and radio journalist and news anchor.[3] The documentary was commissioned by the Maanaw Seva Association, a registered charitable society of Edmonton.[4]

Acharya Dwivedi's initial appointment was only for one year. After completion of the year, he went back to India in December 1990. With the money he earned here, he founded a free school[5] in his village Atsalia in Uttar Pradesh. However, the members of the HSA asked him to continue in his role with the Society. Acharya Dwivedi returned to Edmonton in 1991 and continues as the main priest of the temple.

Acharya Dwivedi was not a professional priest in India. At the HSA, he educates members about the significance of the worship and devotion. He wants worshippers to understand the symbolic meaning of the rituals. Many devotees come to the HCC to listen to his sermons. He is a gifted orator and has perfect Sanskrit pronunciation.

Acharya Dwivedi resided in the temple building with his wife until December 2000, when they had to move to another location due to safety concerns. At this time, the HSA prepared a formal contract with him. In this document, the duties and responsibilities of the priest were laid out as follows:

- Perform ritualistic *pūjā*s in the morning and evening (and/or at additional times as agreed and planned) and

---

3. The trailer of this 54-minute documentary is available on YouTube: https://youtu.be/2_iHcDbMY6U (accessed on July 27, 2019).

4. This society was founded in Edmonton in 1991 by a group of immigrants from India. The founding members of this society were Ramesh Aggarwal, Ashok Bhasin, Jivan Kayande, Harendra Upadhyaya and Dr Jagannath Wani. Except for Mr Bhasin and Dr Wani who were from Calgary, all the other founding members of this organization were members of the HSA.

5. The school is called Srimati Shakuntala Devi Bal Vidyalay, which is named after Acharya Dwivedi's mother. The school has classes 1 to 8.

regular *abhiṣeka* at the temple
- Conduct Sunday worship, festival *pūja*s as required at homes
- Maintain inventory of *pūjā* materials
- Maintain temple area, i.e. appearance and cleanliness
- All above duties are to be performed as per the directions of the Hindu Society of Alberta Vice-President of Programs

Mr Dwivedi's day-off was Saturday. The Society required another priest or a volunteer to perform the rituals on Saturdays, and at other times when the priest was on leave. A position of an assistant priest was thus created in 2014. Mr Bakulesh R. Vyas was the first assistant priest but remained in this role for only sixteen months. Then, Mr Yadav Ram Jha, a Maithil Brahmin from Nepal, was appointed as the assistant priest in September 2016.[6]

---

6. See Appendix B, p. 87, for further details about Mr Jha.

The Kitchen

BEFORE ITS OWN KITCHEN WAS BUILT, the Sikh Society of Alberta amiably allowed the Hindu Society of Alberta to use its kitchen. HSA members would cook at home and bring the food to the temple. The community was much smaller at this time. The construction of the HSA's own kitchen was completed before the formal inauguration of the HCC, and was officially opened on April 8, 1984, with a religious ceremony performed by Mr Kalia. Mr Dev Sharma started this project as Chairman of the kitchen conceptual and layout committee. Mr Ramesh Aggrawal provided support in the form of electricians and electrical material amounting to approximately $12000. Mr P. D. Sarhadi became a life-member of the Society by donating equipment for the kitchen, a significant contribution. The kitchen was originally built where the office rooms are located today. During the fourth phase of the construction, the kitchen was relocated in the basement along with the dining hall.

Activities and Services

OVER ITS FIFTY YEARS OF SERVICE TO THE COMMUNITY, the Hindu Society of Alberta has initiated and hosted many activities and programs, including worship services, celebrations, language classes, yoga classes, and cultural events. The HSA has hosted groups of students from grade schools and universities and raised funds for victims of natural disasters such as the Fort McMurray fire in 2016. President Charu Ranjan (2012–2013) and President Savita Patel (2018–2019) stated that they have enjoyed the variety of programs and events organized by the HSA: religious, non-religious, cultural, both for adults and for children, through their participation on the HSA board over twenty years.

Regular Worship and *Prīti Bhojana*

Before the appointment of the priest, the regular worship, prayer and religious discourses were conducted only on Sundays (9:30 am to 2 pm). Presently, the temple is open every day, and offers both morning and evening worship. From Monday to Friday the temple opens at 8:30 am. The priest performs morning rituals (*pūjā* and *ārati*). The temple closes at 11:30 am and re-opens again from 5:30 pm to 7:30 pm for evening *pūjā* and *ārati*. Morning rituals take place on Saturday from 9 am to 12 noon. The temple remains closed on Saturday and Sunday evenings unless there is a special occasion. The largest attendance is for Sunday prayer. The *pūjā* begins at 10:30 am. After the *pūjā* of the deities, the devotees sing bhajans. Prīti-Bhojana (free vegetarian meal to all visitors) is served on Sunday afternoons. Usually, individual families or groups sponsor the meal. When no sponsor is available, the Society steps in.

Activities and Services

Religious Celebrations

Initially, Dussehra or Vijayā Daśamī and Diwali or Dīpāvali were the two major festivals celebrated by HSA members. As noted earlier, the HSA was in fact founded on a Diwali celebration at Dr Ram Krishan Gupta's home. Over time, many other annual and regular religious festivals and ceremonies were added, such as Śivarātri, Kṛṣṇa-janmāṣṭamī, Rādhāṣṭamī, Holī, Makara-saṅkrānti/Poṅgal, Lohrī, Vasanta-pañcamī, Baisakhi, Buddhajayantī, Mahāvīra-jayantī, Nāga-pañcamī, Navarātri (both autumnal and vernal), Ramakrishna Jayantī, Vivekānanda Jayantī, Nṛsiṃha-caturdaśī, Gaṇeśa-caturthī, Rakṣābandhana, Gītā-jayantī, Satyanārāyaṇapūjā, Durgāpūjā and Dussehra, Kark-caturthī (Karva Chauth), Skanda-ṣaṣṭhī, Śrī Gurunānak Jayantī and Kārtikī Pūrṇimā celebration, Śrī Dattātreya Jayantī, and birthday celebrations of Lord Jesus Christ, Viśvakarma-jayantī, Ādi Śaṅkarācārya Jayantī, Sūryanārāyaṇa-pūjā, Sri Guru Arjun Dev Shaheedi Divas, and others. The first dinner program was held on Diwali in 1972. The fee was $2 per adult. As many as 116 people attended the event, which was honoured by the late Professor Barrington, former ambassador of Burma to Canada.

The thirty-fifth anniversary of the HSA was celebrated at Maharaja Banquet Hall in 2003 during the tenure of Mr Krishan Kumar Chawla. He invited and honoured all the past presidents of the Society. Many ministers attended the program as well. The fortieth anniversary of the HSA was celebrated in Meridian Banquet Hall in October, 2007. Besides members of the HSA and the community at large, many political leaders of all the three levels of the Government attended the event. More than 600 people were present, and the Society raised funds of approximately $50,000.

The fiftieth anniversary was celebrated with the Diwali dinner at the Mirage Banquet Hall on October 13, 2017. Over 500 guests including Members of Legislative Assembly and Members of Parliament attended the event. At the celebration, the founding members were honoured and the Minister of Education, the Honourable David Eggen made a presentation of a cheque in the amount of $24,850 Community Initiative Program grant for the Hindu Society of Alberta History Project.

Non-Religious Celebrations

The Society used to hold non-religious celebrations as well. These included the Independence Day of India (August 15), the Republic Day of India (January 26) and Canada Day (July 1). These events are now organized by the Council of India Societies, and many HSA members continue to take part.

Spiritual Discussions

Since its inception, the HSA has hosted lectures by many spiritual leaders, monks and nuns. By November, 1988, it had received blessings from:

- Jagad Guru Sri Sankaracharya (Sringeri, India);
- Swami Bhashyananda (Ramakrishna order, Chicago, USA);
- Swami Ranganathananda (Ramakrishna Order, India);
- Swami Nishreyasananda (Ramakrishna Order, Rhodesia);
- Swami Satyamitrananda (Haridwar, India);
- Rishi Keshawananda Jee Maharaj (Haridwar, India);
- Brahmrishi Vishwatma Bawra Jee Maharaj, Virat Nagar (Punjab, India);
- Swami Rameshwarananda Giri Maharaj (New Delhi, India);
- Master Sivaya Subramanya (Hawaii, USA);
- Mahamandaleshwar Swami Shivendra (Puri, India);
- Swami Chinmayananda, Sandeepany Sadhanalaya (Bombay, India).

Some exemplary events have included a visit from Sivaya Subramuniaswami, Guru Maha Sannidhanam of Kauai Aadheenam, Hawaii, USA who spoke on "Hindu Solidarity" on October 30, 1983. In 1984, the HSA planned a lecture series on "India's Spiritual Heritage" that included presentations about Hinduism, Buddhism, Sikhism, Jainism, Islam and Christianity. Swami Bhashyananda from Chicago was invited to speak on "Contributions of Swami Vivekananda to World Thought" on February 5, 1984. He delivered another lecture on June 21, 1984. On November 4, 1984, Brahmrishi Vishwatma Bawraji delivered lectures.

Interfaith Activities and Celebrations

Mr Sushil Kumar Kalia was a member of the Interfaith Society of Edmonton. Through this connection, the HSA participated in many interfaith dialogues and programs. The City of Edmonton, in collaboration with the Interfaith Society of Edmonton, began a monthly celebration of different religious festivals. As part of this initiative, The City of Edmonton first declared the Hindu faith's festival month by allowing Hindu Society of Alberta to organize a Diwali celebration at City Hall on October 20, 2006. The mayor of Edmonton, the Honourable Stephen Mandel, inaugurated the celebration.

Sometime in 1984 or 1985, the Ahmadiyya Moslem Association organized a Religious Founders Day Symposium, in which Mr Kalia presented a paper on Sri Krishna. Mrs Indira Arora represented the Society in the interfaith religion meeting, and her presentation was well received.

The HSA itself has hosted many Interfaith Dialogues. On March 8, 2003, an Interfaith Dialogue was held at the HCC on Saṃskāras: Sacred Sacraments of Purificatory Rites of Passage. Lama Lian Nei, David Goa, Sushil K. Kalia, Evelyn Hamdon, Jitendra A. Shah, Awatar Singh Sekhon and Firdosh Mehta presented on Buddhism, Christianity, Hinduism, Islam, Jainism, Sikhism and Zoroastrianism respectively. A Dialogue on Roles and Rituals of Women was held at the HSA on March 5, 2005. Ms Kirsten Goa, Ms Jagjeet Bhardwaj, Ms Shayda Nanji, Ms Devila Mehta and Ms. Harinder Malhotra presented on Christianity, Hinduism, Islam, Jainism and Sikhism respectively.

The HSA also participates in interfaith gatherings held by other community organization to increase the awareness and understanding of the faiths represented in the Capital Region. In 2015 and 2016, the delegations consisted of Renu Narang, Jignesh Gadhia, Hansa Thaleshvar, Manoj Kumar Gupta, Deepak Lama, Renuka Ghimire and Pranov Lama.

Cultural Programs

Since its inception, the HSA and its members have played an active role in promoting arts from the Indian sub-continent. In the late 1970s, the HSA hosted a program on Indian music called *Sangam* on Quality Cable FM 99.1 every Wednesday from 9 pm to 10 pm. Hosts for the program were Vinod Ratti and Lok Sharma.

Although performance artists were not invited directly by the HSA, HSA members were active in inviting artists and making necessary arrangements. Masood Ahmad, a librarian in the Department of Mathematics, University of Alberta, was often invited to play tabla. Mr Chris Balchandra and his wife Mrs Ramona Balchandra would perform at HSA events even on short notice. Mr Balchandra was a versatile singer and an instrumentalist. Mrs Balchandra was a dancer who took great pleasure in dancing to the music of her husband. Both husband and wife worked at the same school not far from Edmonton.

Many members of the HSA were directly involved with the Edmonton Raga-mala Music Society, which was formed in 1983.[1] The Raga-mala Society promotes and hosts classical

---

1. The Raga-mala Society was started in Calgary. Dr Ratnakar Gosavi was one of the founders.

Activities and Services

music and dances from the Indian sub-continent. Many members of the HSA, such as Dr Mangesh Ganesh Murdeshwar, his wife Mrs Maya Murdeshwar, Dr Sujit Kumar Chakrabartty, his wife Mrs Aruna Chakrabartty, their daughter Ms Shreela Chakrabartty, Mr Gajanan Pundit, Mrs Devayani Pundit, their daughter Mrs Shirish Chotalia, Mr Kumud Acharya, Mrs Charu Ranjan, her husband Mr Rajiv Ranjan were or are presently actively involved in the Edmonton Raga-mala Music Society. Mr Murdeshwar himself was a great singer and performed several times at the HCC.

The HSA has organised several musical concerts and performances over the years, including a sitar recital by Ravi Shankar, classical dances by Padmini and Ragini and by the late Pt. Gopi Krishna, and singing by the late Hemant Kumar. For many years, Mrs Nimmi Sanon was responsible for organizing these programs. Some additional highlights have included:

- Sometime between October 1, 1972 and September 30, 1973, the HSA held a Punjabi cultural program and Anjali dances.
- Sometime between October 1973 and September 1974 the HSA held a musical concert by the renowned classical musician Chitti Babu, a Bharatanatyam performance by the celebrated dancer Padmini, a Qawwali program, and a multicultural show.
- On the occasion of the Foundation Stone Ceremony of the HCC on August 7, 1976, there were dance performances by Kanan Amin, Shreelekha Mehta and Aditi Mehta, Bhajan by Mr Kapileshwari, Sucheta Rao, Navas and Shafik (both from Uganda), songs by Abha Sharma and Lok Sharma, and group folk songs performed by Prema, Shyama, Bharati, Kamala, Abha and Mrs Pandit.
- The HSA organized a sarod recital by Aashish Khan with his brother Pranesh Khan on tabla (grandsons of Allauddin Khan) on June 3, 1979. The recital took place

in the Humanities Building, University of Alberta.
- On July 14, 1979, the Society organized a special music presentation, "Folk Music of India" by Bhupen Hazarika. The event was held at the Humanities Building, University of Alberta.
- The HSA organized a concert of Hindustani music, both vocal and instrumental, lead by Vinod Bhardwaj and Lok Sharma on November 12, 1983.
- The Society hosted the Saint Tyāgarāja Ārādhanā celebrations organized by the Edmonton Tamil Cultural Association in May 1984. Facilities to celebrate the Purandaradāsa Ārādhanā festival were also provided to the same organization.
- On May 4, 1985 an evening of devotional music (Sanskrit *bhajana-sandhyā*) was presented by Dr Mangesh Murdeshwar, one of the founding members of the HSA, and Suchetha Rao.
- Sometime between April 1985 and March 1986, an event called "A Celebration of the Arts of India" was held at the Edmonton Art Gallery. The HSA and the Edmonton Art Gallery organized this program of Indian classical dances and music in conjunction with the Hindu Sculptures Exhibition at the gallery. The program ended with a reception and tour of the Hindu exhibition. The event was attended by dignitaries including Horst Schmid, Minister of Tourism, Alderman and Mrs Terry Kavanagh, and Mr Arnall from the office of the Secretary of State. Sikh, Ismaili, and Edmonton Multicultural Society community leaders were present, as were guests from the City of Edmonton, Alberta Culture and other government departments. Nalayinie Sivakumaran performed Bharatanatyam. There was a sitar recital by Seema Ganatra, and vocal music by Lok Sharma, Abha Sharma, Kapil Gurtu, Punam Gurtu, Anil Bates, Ranjana Bates, Achala Seth, and Vinodh Bhardwaj. Prem Tiwari accompanied on tabla. There was

Activities and Services

also a violin recital by Lewis Davies. To commemorate the event, a twelve-page program souvenir containing articles on Indian music and sculptures was released.

- To mark the 20th anniversary of the HSA, the Society organized two cultural events on October 11 and November 21, 1987 at the Convention Centre and the Provincial Museum Auditorium respectively. The first event was a musical evening by Padmashree K. J. Yesudas accompanied by Hari Prasad Chaurasia on flute, Pandit Shiv Kumar Sharma on santoor and Prof. V. G. Jog on violin. The Edmonton Raga-mala Music Society, Spice Village and Alberta's Wild Rose Foundation co-sponsored this event with the HSA. The other event was a Bharatanatyam performance by renowned artist Allarmel Valli.
- On October 28, 1989, the HSA organized a cultural program of folk music (Garba and Rajasthani), classical music (Odissi, Kathak and Bharatanatyam), and devotional music (Bhajans) with accompanying dances. The event was held in the Provincial Museum Auditorium. Various other organizations participated in this program. Members of Bengali Association, Alberta Gujarati Cultural Association and Alberta Hindi Parishad performed instrumental music, Garba dance (a folk dance from western India) and group dance respectively. This program included a group song by children as well.
- A charity show of songs and dances from popular Hindi films was organized by Dr Sunil Datar with the assistance of Lalita Koodoo and Nimmi Sanon, who was President of the HAS at that time. Proceeds from the show, held on September 23, 2000 at the Citadel Theatre, supported renovation and enhancement of the HCC.
- The City of Edmonton declared October 20–27, 2006 as Deepawali Week. The HSA was given the opportunity to display educational material and exhibits for the

celebrations. A week-long public exhibition at Edmonton's City Hall was open daily.
- On November 7, 2015, the HSA organized a concert of old and new Hindi songs at the Capilano Conference Centre as a part of the Diwali festival. The singers were Ashif Jeria and Yuthika Varma.

Publication of Magazine and Souvenirs

Over the years, the Society has produced regular newsletters, and occasional themed magazines and souvenir publications. The first of such souvenirs was on the occasion of the Foundation Stone Ceremony of the Hindu Cultural Centre on August 7, 1976. On May 21, 1983, the *Panch Devta Pran Pratishtha Souvenir* was published to commemorate the installation of the *mūrti*s of five deities (Pañca Devatā). Another souvenir magazine was published on September 15, 1984, documenting the opening ceremony of the Hindu Cultural Centre. A short souvenir was published on June 19, 1988 for the portrait inauguration of Guru Nanak and Sathya Sai Baba. There was a *20th Anniversary and Deepawali Celebration* souvenir publication on November 9, 1988. Most of its contents were reproductions of articles from Bharatiya Vidya Bhavan's journals. On March 19, 1989, the *Jain Pratishtha Mahotsava Souvenir Issue* was published on the occasion of the installation of the marble murtis of Lord Mahāvīra.

The first magazine of the HSA, entitled the *Hindu Society Magazine*, was published in June 1979 with the initiative of Mr Brahma Swaroop Varma. He was the chief editor of the magazine, while Mr Sushil Kumar Kalia served as editor. Magazines were theme-based. For example, the themes for the first (June 1979) and the second issues (July 1979) were Ādi Śaṅkarācārya and Goddess Sarasvatī respectively. Early magazine publications were irregular.

Regular annual publication of the HSA magazine began in the first half of the 1990s. The magazine was named

Patrika. Mr Sushil Kumar Kalia edited *Patrika* until 2004. Mr Rajiv Ranjan Chaturvedi edited three issues of *Patrika*— the 2004–2005 issue, the 2005–2006 issue and the 2006–2007 issue. Mr Kumud Acharya has since edited further issues of the magazine. *Patrika* contains writings on various topics, short literary pieces by members, and occasional excerpts from Hindu religious or philosophical literature. It also includes a list of the life members of the Society along with their phone numbers. The Society generates revenue by publishing advertisements in *Patrika*.

Library Facility

The HCC houses a library full of books on scriptures, history and philosophy. Most of the books are in English and Hindi. A few are in Gujarati and Punjabi. The library has been in use since the early 1980s. The establishment of the library was initiated by a dedicated couple, Mrs Vijay Parkash and her husband Mr Sat Parkash. The couple worked hard to organize a book lending service and procure new titles. Later, due to ill health, Mrs Parkash could help for only a short time but her husband Sat Parkash carried on with this voluntary service. In 1983–1984, Mr Satya Bhardwaj served as the librarian, and Mr Parveen Kalra was the library coordinator.

At the occasion of the silver jubilee celebrations of the Society, the library was formally inaugurated by Brahm Rishi Bawra Jee, an Indian saint and scholar. The library was dedicated to the community and named the Dr Sat Parkash Library.

Over time, the Society has invested considerably in the library collection. For example, in 1993–1994 and in 1996–1997, the Society spent $1272 and $2893 respectively on books. Mr Sushil Kalia and Mr Naresh Sharma helped to obtain government grants for this purpose. In the years 1993–1994, Dr Naresh Jha and his team were instrumental in revitalizing the library. Many books were donated by members of the Society and other supporting groups. By this time, there were already over 1,500 books on various subjects.

Initially, the library was situated in the room adjacent to the main entrance, where the toilets exist today. During the expansion project in 2004–2005, the library was relocated to the boardroom next to the office. However, by this time there was no librarian and no provisions for loaning books. In 2015 and 2016, Mrs Meera Mittra, Mr Desh Mittra and many other volunteers undertook a great effort to organize the library's collection. Mrs Mittra was a professional cataloguer who worked as a cataloguing supervisor in the Peace Library System. Mr and Mrs Mittra and volunteers worked hard to prepare a digital catalogue of all books. Two bookshelves were purchased, and the books on religion were placed there. Other books and reference material were placed inside the smaller room.

At the present time, the library is not functional due to a lack of human and financial resources. Visitors to the HCC sometimes do go to the library and use the books there. Individuals looking for reference material also search the collection but there is no one available on the premises to help the visitors.

Other Ad Hoc Classes and Services

As interest and opportunity arise from time to time, the Society organizes various learning sessions or classes.

Language Classes

In the past, weekly activities of the HSA included language classes for community members. Hindi, Sanskrit, and Bengali were taught. In 1978, the HSA received government grants of $292.50 and $216 for conducting Hindi and Bengali language classes respectively. In 1979, the grants were $718 and $224. The 1979 edition of the *Hindu Society Magazine* (Vol. 1, No. 2) indicates that the weekly Hindi and Bengali classes took place on Saturdays at 11:00 am. Dr Ambikeshwar Sharma and Mrs Aruna Chakrabartty conducted the Hindi and the Bengali classes respectively, using the Education Building of the University of Alberta. In 1985–1986, Mrs Neelam Rai and Mrs Madhu Sehgal assisted Dr Sharma. For his ongoing work, Dr Sharma received the Language Heritage Award from the Government of Alberta. In 1985, Alberta Hindi Parishad began to offer language instruction, and consequently in a few years the HSA discontinued its Hindi classes. According to Mr Kalia, the Hindi Parishad is a product of these earlier initiatives by the HSA. The Bengali classes, too, were discontinued by the mid-1980s, as the Edmonton Bengali Association began offering Bengali language class.

The Society also offered language classes to children under an initiative called Bal Sabha (see below). For a period in the 1990s, Sanskrit classes conducted by Acharya Shiv Shankar Dwivedi were offered every Monday from 6:30 pm to 7:30 pm.

Charter Flight (1968–1969)

In the first summer after its establishment, the Society arranged charter flights for members who wished to travel to India. This service was offered in 1968 and in 1969. At that time, the Government of Canada permitted such charters to specific groups for their members. Mr Asgar Ali was the co-ordinator in 1968 and Dr S. P. Khetarpal became the coordinator in 1969. Through this service, the Society acquired members from Saskatoon, Winnipeg and Calgary and rural areas of Alberta. Members paid $1 to join the Society and avail themselves of the charter service. The Society received a $250 reimbursement from the travel agent for arranging these group flights.

Religious and Spiritual Classes

Over the years the HSA has organized religious and spiritual classes for its members. Religious classes were introduced to enlighten members about ways to achieve peace and happiness in life. Acharya Shiv Shankar Dwivedi conducted these classes. Mr Dwivedi also taught the application and significance of various Hindu mantras, such as the Gāyatrī Mantra, the Mahāmṛtyuñjaya Mantra, and the Mahālakṣmī Mantra. At some point, the Society also began to offer yoga classes for members. These classes continue be offered periodically, offering such topics as Pranayama, posture and relaxation. There have also been sessions held on weekday afternoons for discussing and debating various topics related to Hinduism.

Bal Sabha

The HSA carries out a number of activities for children under the banner Bal Sabha (Children's Assembly), which initially included Hindi language classes and religious classes. In January 1984, Hindi classes began as part of the program. Classes were held on Sundays for two hours. In 1984, the coordinators of Bal Sabha were Mrs Saroj Bhardwaj, Mrs Indira Arora and Mrs Sarla Sarhadi. In 1985–1986, the language classes were conducted by Mrs Sarita Puri and then Bal Sabha coordinator Mrs Janak Kalia. Sessions were discontinued until Mrs Renu Narang and Mrs Malti Aroa helped to revive the Bal Sabha again in 1994.

Music and Dance Classes

When the HSA held their Sunday gathering at the 10436–81 Avenue location, Indian music and dance classes were offered. In the mid-1970s, Malavika Malviya came from Bombay and taught Indian classical dances for at least two years. Her area of focus was Kuchipudi. Vocalist Chandrakant Kapileshwari and Bharatanatyam artists Shreelekha Mehta and Aditi Mehta from Mumbai were the first artists-in-residence between 1978–1979. They started formal music and dance instruction in Edmonton that served the entire Indian community and sparked a love of Indian classical arts amongst Edmontonians. On Sundays, the classes would take place in the afternoon in the same room where members of the HSA held their sessions in the morning. Mrs Shyam Pundit's daughter, Mrs Shrishti Nigam hosted Mr Chandrakant Kapileshwari during his stay in Edmonton. The next artists-in-residence were Aashish and Pranesh Khan (sarod & tabla) in 1979. They stayed in peoples' homes and taught music over the summer. After the Mehta sisters left in 1979, Shyamala Nagendran from Sri Lanka took over. She was the first permanent resident and Canadian citizen to establish Bharatanatyam dance instruction in Edmonton. There were other occasional music and dance classes offered at the HCC. During the mid-1980s, Mrs Nalayinie Sivakumaran offered regular dance classes, but after this period, no regular music or dance classes were held at the facility.

Connection with Other Non-Governmental Organizations

UPON ITS ESTABLISHMENT, the HSA became the point of contact for the Indian community in Edmonton. When the Council of India Societies was formed, the HSA joined as a member organisation. Many other Indian societies were and are presently assisted by the HSA, and many members of the HSA are members of those other societies. In turn, these societies contributed financially to the HSA. The HSA took part in the meeting for the formation of Hindu Council of Canada, which was organized by the Vishva Hindu Parishad of British Columbia in 1987. Mr Sushil Kumar Kalia along with three other members represented the Society.

The Vedanta Society of Edmonton (VSE) has been using the Swami Vivekananda Hall of the HCC for a number of years and makes donations for use of the space. The HSA has benefitted when the VSE as invited special guests, visiting from other cities. All the founding members of the VSE are also members of the HSA. Moreover, the HCC is the official address of the Jain Society of Alberta. The HSA has periodically worked with Alberta Hindi Parishad, Shanti Niketan, the Edmonton Tamil Cultural Association, the Telugu Cultural Association of Edmonton, the Society of Friends of Nepal, the Sindhi Association of Alberta, Marathi Bhashik Mandal Edmonton, the Maanav Seva Association, the Jain Society of Edmonton, the Maha Ganapati Society of Alberta, Saiva Siddhanta Church Edmonton Mission, the Kerala Bhajan Group, the Prem Society, Brahma Kumaris Edmonton Centre, the Caribbean Hindu Association, the Edmonton Ramayan Geeta Congregation, the Sanatan Society of Alberta, the Andhra Cultural Association, the Kannada Cultural Association of Alberta, the Alberta Gujarati Association, the Edmonton Bengali Association, Sri Sathya Sai Baba

Centre of Edmonton, the Canada India Youth Association, the Indo Canadian Association, the Asian Youth Club, the Wild Rose Society for Preservation of the Traditional Art, the MCF Multicultural Communications Foundation, the Parbasi Multicultural Society, the Bharatiya Cultural Society of Alberta, the Edmonton Raga-mala Music Society and the Jhankar Society for Dance and Music.

Appendix A: Past Executives and Boards

The names of all board members of the following years could unfortunately not be traced: 1968–1969, 1969–1970, 1970–1971, 1971–1972, 1972–1973, 1976–1977, 1977–1978, 1978–1979, 1979–1980, 1980–1981, 1981–1982 and 1992–1993.

For about the first seven years, the leadership position in the Society was that of a General Secretary (not President) and the Executive Committee was limited to five members.

1967–1968

General Secretary	Dr Ram Krishan Gupta
Members	Mr Gajanan Pundit
	Mr Baldev Raj Abbi
	Mr J. N. Sherman
	Mr Vidyasagar

1968–1969

General Secretary : Dr Ram Krishan Gupta

1969–1970

General Secretary   Dr Ram Krishan Gupta

1970–1971

General Secretary   Dr Ram Krishan Gupta

Appendix A: Past Executives and Boards

1971–1972

General Secretary   Dr Raghavendra Yamdagni

1972–1973

General Secretary   Mr Uday Bagwe[1]

1973–1974

General Secretary	Mrs Maya Murdeshwar
Joint Secretary	Dr P. M. Rao
Treasurer	Dr M. L. Khandekar
Members	Dr Ram K. Gupta
	Dr N. C. Das
	Dr Datta G. Salgaonkar
	Dr Raghav Yamdagni

1974–1975

President	Mr Krishan Chandra Joshee
General Secretary	Dr Kamal Nath Jha
VP Provisional (HCC)	Dr Ram K. Gupta
Joint Secretary	Mr Vishvabandhu Juneja
Treasurer	Dr Vinod K. Ratti
Members	Mr Shyam Behari
	Mrs Sheela Joshi
	Mr Asit K. Hazra

1975–1976

President	Dr Kamal Nath Jha
General Secretary	Dr P. M. Rao

---

1. In 1972, Dr Mangesh Ganesh Murdeshwar became the General Secretary. However, he resigned in the middle of his term and Mr Bagwe carried his term to completion.

Board of Directors
Program Committee
- Chairman: Mr V. Juneja
- Secretary: Mrs N. Sanon
- Treasurer: Dr R. D. Mehta
- Directors: Dr V. K. Ratti
  - Mr K. K. Chawla
  - Mr M. Prasad
  - Mr N. Sharma

Cultural Center Committee
- Chairman: Dr R. K. Gupta
- Secretary: Dr K. L. Mehra
- Treasurer: Dr S. Chakrabartty
- Directors: Mr K. C. Joshee
  - Dr B. K. Sinha
  - Dr S. Varma

1976–1977

President   Mr Krishan Chandra Joshee

1977–1978

President   Dr Kamal Nath Jha

1978–1979

President   Mr Krishan Chandra Joshee

1979–1980

President   Dr Kamal Nath Jha

1980–1981

(Programs Committee)
Chairman	Mr Jivan Kayande
Secretary	Mr Sushil K. Kalia
Treasurer	Mr Krishan K. Chawla
Members	Mr Brahma S. Varma
	Dr Ram D. Mehta
	Mr Madan M. Prasad
	Mrs Sandhya Bagwe
	Mr Bishambhar Trikha
	Mr Surinder K. Sachdev
Co-opted Members	Mr Madatali Lalani
	Mr Lok Sharma
	Mr Ram Sharma
	Mr Bhanubhai Joshi

1981–1982

President   Dr Kamal Nath Jha

1982–1983

President	Mr K. C. Joshee
General Secretary	Mr Pitambar Lal Avasthi
Program Committee	
Chairman	Mr Madan M. Prasad
Secretary	Mr Sushil Kumar Kalia
Treasurer	Mr Ved Gupta
Members	Mr N. K. Panjwani
	Mr Kapil Gurtu
	Mr Dev Sharma
	Mr Mohan Juneja
	Mr Narain Khemchandani
Cultural Centre Committee	
Chairman	Dr Ram K. Gupta

Secretary	Mr Brahma S. Varma
Treasurer	Dr Sujit K. Chakrabartty
Members	Mr K. K. Sanon
	Mr Jivan Kayande
	Mr P. D. Sarhadi
Shrine Committee	
Chairman	Mr Sushil K. Kalia
Members	Dr Sujit K. Chakrabartty
	Mr K. K. Sanon
Building Committee	
Chairman	Mr K. K. Sanon
Members	Dr Ram K. Gupta
	Dr Sujit K. Chakrabartty
	Mr Sushil K. Kalia
Cultural Activities	Mr Kapil Gurtu
Bal Sabha	Mrs Saroj Bhardwaj
	Mrs Sarla Sarhadi
Religious Activities	Mr Sushil K. Kalia

1983–1984

President	Dr Ram Krishan Gupta
	Mr K. C. Joshee (after Dr Gupta's resignation)[2]
General Secretary	Mr Madan M. Prasad
VP Administration	Mr K. K. Sanon
VP Programs	Mr Sushil Kumar Kalia
Treasurer	Mr Pitambar Avasthi
Directors	Mr Ramesh Aggarwal
	Mr Ved P. Gupta
	Mr Jivan Kayande
	Mr Narain Khemchandani
	Mr Ramesh C. Khullar

---

2. Before completion of the term, Dr Gupta resigned from the HSA board on personal grounds. The Board accepted the resignation at the Board meeting held on September 25, 1983. Thereafter, Mr K. C. Joshee worked as the Acting President

Appendix A: Past Executives and Boards

	Mr M. N. Mehrotra
	Mr Niranjan Panjwani
	Mr P. D. Sarhadi
	Mr Dev Sharma
	Mr Bhajan Uttamchandani
Bal Sabha	Mrs Saroj Bhardwaj
	Mrs Sarla Sarhadi
Auditors	Mr Sujit K. Chakrabartty
	Mr Sat Parkash

1984–1985

Past President	Mr K. K. Sanon
President	Mr K. C. Joshee
VP Administration	Mr P. D. Sarhadi
VP Programs	Mr Sushil Kumar Kalia
Treasurer	Mr Pitambar Avasthi
General Secretary	Mr Sujit Kumar Chakrabartty
Directors	Mr Ramesh Aggarwal
	Mr Ramesh Chandra Kullar
	Mr Dev Sharma
	Mr Bhajan Uttamchandani
	Mrs Saroj Bhardwaj
	Mr Sat Prakash
	Mr Arjun Singh
	Mr Amar Bhasin
	Mr Dinesh Puri
	Mr Ram Dev Mehta
Auditors	Mr Kishan Katyal
	Mr Bhagirath Singh

1985–1986

Past President	Mr Krishan C. Joshee
President	Mr Sushil Kumar Kalia

VP Administration	Mr Ramesh C. Khullar
Joint Secretary	Mr Brahma S. Varma
VP Programs	Mr Jivan A. Kayande
Joint Secretary	Mr Arjun Singh
General Secretary	Mr Madan Mohan Prasad
Treasurer	Mr Ramesh Aggarwal
Asst. Treasurer	Mr Niranjan K. Panjwani
Directors	Mr Pitambar L. Avasthi
	Mr Raj Kumar Bagga
	Mr Amar Bhasin
	Mr Ashwini Kumar Bhasin
	Mr Kailash Chawla
	Mr Ratnakar Gosavi
	Mrs Janak Kalia
Auditors	Mr Viren Bhatnagar
	Mr Naresh Bibra

1986–1987

Past President	Mr Sushil Kumar Kalia
President	Mr Ramesh Chander Khullar
VP Administration	Mr Brahma Swaroop Varma
Joint Secretary	Mr Ashwini Bhasin
VP Programs	Mr Kailash Chawla
Joint Secretary	Mr Jivan Kayande
General Secretary	Dr Ratnakar Gosavi
Joint Secretary	Mr Madan Mohan Prasad
Treasurer	Mr Pitambar Lal Avasthi
Asst. Treasurer	Mr V. K. Bhatnagar
Directors	Mrs Janak Kalia
	Dr N. K. Gupta
	Mr Naresh Sharma
	Mr Raj Bagga
	Mr Vijay Sawhney
	Mr Balwant Gandhi
Auditors	Dr Krishan Katyal

Appendix A: Past Executives and Boards

Dr Bhagirath Singh

1987–1988

Past President	Mr R. C. Khullar
President	Mr Pitambar L. Avasthi
VP Administration	Mr Brahma Swarup Varma
VP Programs	Mr Naresh Sharma
General Secretary	Mr Madan Mohan Prasad
Treasurer	Mr Ramesh Aggarwal
Directors	Mrs Indira Arora
	Mr Virendra Bhatnagar
	Mr Balvant Gandhi
	Mr Sushil Kumar Kalia
	Mr Krishan Lal Katyal
	Mr Jivan Kayande
	Mr Braj Behari Prasad
	Mr Kewal K. Sanon
	Mr Satish C. Sehgal
	Mr Arjun Singh
Auditors	Ms Anuradha Gosavi
	Mr Vijay Sharma

1988–1989

Past President	Mr Pitambar L. Avasthi
President	Mr Madan Mohan Prasad
VP Administration	Mr Naresh Sharma
VP Programs	Mr K. K. Sanon
General Secretary	Mr Lok Sharma
Treasurer	Mr Krishan Lal Katyal
Directors	Mr Baldev Abbi
	Mr Ramesh Aggarwal
	Mr Parmod Bawa
	Mr Ashvin M. Bilimoria
	Mr Anil Dhar

	Mr Ratnakar Gosavi
	Mr Sushil Kumar Kalia
	Mrs Kiran Mehra
	Mr Satish C. Sehgal
	Mrs Tara Shah
Auditors	Mr Bhagirath Singh
	Mr R. L. Singh

1989–1990

Past President	Mr Madan Mohan Prasad
President	Mr Jivan Kayande
VP Administration	Mr Ratnakar Gosavi
VP Programs	Mr Sushil Kumar Kalia
General Secretary	Mr Balvant A. Gandhi
Treasurer	Mr Parmod Bawa
Directors	Mr Ramesh Aggarwal
	Mr Rajesh Dhir
	Mr Anil Garg
	Mrs Kiran Mehra
	Mrs Nirmal Sanon
	Mr M. P. Sharma
	Mr R. L. Singh
	Mr S. P. Singh
	Mr Shantaram Woosaree
Auditors	Mr M. K. Jain
	Mr K. K. Chawla

1990–1991

President	Dr K. L. Katyal
VP Administration	Mr Ramesh Aggarwal
VP Programs	Mrs Nirmal (Nimmi) Sanon
General Secretary	Mr Anil Dhar
Treasurer	Mr Parmod Bawa
Past President	Mr Jivan Kayande

Appendix A: Past Executives and Boards

Directors	Mr Balvant Gandhi
	Dr M. P. Sharma
	Mr Bhanu Joshi
	Mr Raj Bagga
	Mr Madan Prasad
	Mrs Sita Prasad
	Mr Raj Shorey
	Mr H. S. Upadhyay
	Mr Brahma Varma
	Mr Viren Bhatnagar
Auditors	Dr M. K. Jain
	Dr Bhagirath Singh

1991–1992

President	Mr Balvant A. Gandhi
VP Administration	Mr Baldev Abbi
VP Programs	Mr Brahma Swarup Varma
General Secretary	Mrs Kiran Mehra
Treasurer	Mr Bhanubhai Joshi
Past President	Mr Krishan Katyal
Directors	Mr Robin Chakravorty
	Mr Sujit Chakrabartty
	Mr Sunil Channan
	Mrs Anuradha Gosavi
	Mr Subhash Khullar
	Mr Ashok Malhotra
	Mrs Poonam Mehra
	Mr Mahendra Mehta
	Mrs Tara Shah
Auditors	Mr Anil Garg
	Mr Ratnakar Gosavi

1992–1993

President   Mr Brahma Swaroop Varma

1993–1994

President	Mrs Poonam Mehra
Vice-President	Mr Amar Bhasin
Vice-President	Mr Prem Kharbanda
General Secretary	Mr Balvant Gandhi
Treasurer	Dr Krishan Katyal
Past President	Mr Brahma Swarup Varma
Directors	Mr Vinod Bhardwaj
	Mr Vimal Bhatia
	Mr Ratnakar Gosavi
	Mr Mr Suresh Jani
	Mr Jivan Kayande
	Mr Arvind Kapur
	Mr Jivan Mistry
	Mr Madan Prasad
	Mr Vijay Sawhney
	Mr Naresh Sharma
Auditors	Mr Raj Shorey
	Mr Bhanubhai Joshi

1995–1996

President	Mr Bhanu Bhai Joshi
VP Management	Mr Amar Nath Bhasin
VP Programs	Mr Jivan Kayande
General Secretary	Mr Suresh Jani
Treasurer	Mr Vimal Bhatia
Past President	Mrs Poonam Mehra
Director	Mr Raj Bagga
	Mr Vinod Bhardwaj
	Mr Balvant Gandhi

Appendix A: Past Executives and Boards 71

Auditors	Mr Sushil Kalia Mr Krishan Katyal Mr Vijay Sawhney Naresh Sharma Subash Sikka Mrs Indira Pandya Mr Madan M. Prasad

1996–1997

President	Mr Amar Bhasin
VP Administration	Mr Vijay Sawhney
VP Programs	Mr Jivan Kayande
Secretary	Mrs Renu Narang
Co-secretary	Mr Krishan Bukka
Treasurer	Mr Vimal Bhatia
Past President	Mr Bhanu Bhai Joshi
Directors	Mr Vinod Bhardwaj
	Mr Balvant Gandhi
	Mr Kapil Gurtu
	Mr Sushil Kalia
	Mr Krishan Katyal
	Mr Anup Khanna
	Mr Vijay Malhotra
	Mr Tara Mistry
	Mr Tej Nand
	Mr Om P. Rajora
	Mrs Sarla Sarhadi
	Mr Naresh Sharma

1997–1998

President	Mr Jivan Kayande
VP Administration	Mr Bhanubhai Joshi
VP Programs	Mr Tej Kaur Nand

General Secretary	Mr Om P. Rajora
Treasurer	Mr Anup Khanna
Past President	Mr Amar Bhasin
Directors	Mr Pitamber Avasthi
	Mr Vimal Bhatia
	Mrs Monica Bhasin
	Mr Krishna Bukka
	Mr Vijay Malhotra
	Mr Babulal Mehta
	Ms Tara Mistry
	Ms Sarla Sarhadi
	Mr Vijay Sawhney
	Mr Shiv Saraswat
Auditors	Mr Balvant Gandhi
	Ms Purnima Prasad

1998–1999

President	Mr Sushil Kumar Kalia
VP Administration	Mr Naresh Chandra Sharma
VP Programs	Mr Prem Kharbanda
General Secretary	Mr Om P. Rajora
Treasurer	Mr Krishna Bukka
Past President	Jivan Kayande
Directors	Mrs Sandhya Bagwe
	Mr Balwant Gandhi
	Mr Venkat Hegde
	Mr Krishan Katyal
	Mr Anup Khanna
	Mr Satbir Khatri
	Mr M. N. Mehrotra
	Mr Babulal Mehta
	Mrs Savita Patel
	Mr Someshwar Sharma
Auditors	Mr M. K. Jain
	Mr Madan M. Prasad

Appendix A: Past Executives and Boards

1999–2000

President	Mr Vimal Bhatia
VP Administration	Mr Amar Bhasin
VP Programs	Mrs Savita Patel
General Secretary	Mr Bhanu Bhai Joshi
Treasurer	Mr Amar Khanna
Past President	Mr Sushil Kumar Kalia
Directors	Mrs Anjali Agarwal
	Mrs Krishna Bukka
	Mr Krish Dhunnoo
	Mr Balwant Gandhi
	Mr Narendra Gogna
	Mr Mahendra Jain
	Mr Prem Kharbana
	Mr Babu Lal Mehta
	Mr Vivek Pathak
	Dr Om Rajora
	Mrs Nimmi Sanon
	Mrs Pooja Sawhney
	Mr Vijay Sawhney
	Mrs Susheela Subbarao
Auditors	Mr Jivan Kayande
	Mr Madan Mohan Prasad

2000–2001

President	Mrs Nimmi Sanon
VP Administration	Mrs Monica Bhasin
VP Programs	Mr Sushil Kumar Kalia
General Secretary	Mrs Anjali Agarwal
Treasurer	Mr Bhanu Bhai Joshi
Past President	Mr Vimal Bhatia
Directors	Mrs Sandhya Bagwe
	Mr Amar Bhasin
	Mr Nitin Bhatia
	Mr Krish Dhunnoo

	Mr Prem Kharbanda
	Mr Surendra Kotak
	Mr Vinod Marwah
	Mr Mool Mehrotra
	Mrs Savita Patel
	Mrs Veena Sawhney
Auditors	Mr Jivan Kayande
	Mr Madan Prasad

2001–2002

President	Mr Naresh Sharma
VP Administration	Mr Balwant Gandhi
VP Programs	Mr Sushil Kumar Kalia
General Secretary	Ms Anjali Agarwal
Treasurer	Mr Tej K. Nand
Past President	Ms Nimmi Sanon
Directors	Ms Sandhya Bagwe
	Mr Krishan Chawla
	Mr Krish Dhunnoo
	Mr Anil Garg
	Ms Jyoti Gupta
	Mr Bhanu Bhai Joshi
	Ms Shashi Kalia
	Mr Krishan K. Katyal
	Mr Surinder Kotak
	Mr Vinod Marwaha
	Ms Poonam Mehra
	Ms Savita Patel
	Ms Charu Ranjan
	Mr Satish Sehgal
	Mr M. P. Sharma
	Mr Preetam Sharma
	Mr R. J. Singh
Auditors	Mr M. K. Jain
	Mr Madan M. Prasad

Appendix A: Past Executives and Boards

2002–2003

President	Mr Krishan K. Chawla
VP Administration	Mr Preetam Sharma
VP Programs	Ms Charu Ranjan
General Secretary	Mrs Anjali Agarwal
Treasurer	Mr Anil Garg
Past President	Mr Naresh Sharma
Directors	Ms Sandhya Bagwe
	Mrs Niru Channan
	Ms Anubha Gupta
	Ms Jyoti Gupta
	Mr Sushil K. Kalia
	Mr Krishan K. Katyal
	Mr Vinod Marwaha
	Ms Poonam Mehra
	Ms Savita Patel
	Mr Satish Sehgal
	Mr Gulshan Sethi
	Mr M. P. Sharma
	Mr R. L Singh
	Mr Rajeshwar Singh
Auditors	Mr Raj Bansal
	Mr Jivan Kayande

2003–2004

President	Mr Krishan K. Chawla
VP Administration	Mr Preetam Sharma
VP Programs	Ms Charu Ranjan
General Secretary	Mr M. P. Sharma
Treasurer	Mr Rajeshwar Singh
Past President	Mr Naresh Sharma
Directors	Ms Anjali Agarwal
	Ms Sandhya Bagwe
	Mr Raj Bansal

	Mrs Niru Channan
	Mr Bhanubhai Joshi
	Mr Sushil Kalia
	Mr Kishan Katyal
	Mr Jivan Kayande
	Mr Surendra Kotak
	Mr Vinod Marwah
	Mr Mool Mehrotra
	Mr Suresh Patel
	Mr Satish Sehgal
	Mr R. L. Singh
Auditors	Mr Rohit Desai
	Ms Sarla Sharma

2004–2005

President	Mr Preetam Sharma
VP Administration	Mrs Niru Channan
VP Programs	Mrs Charu Ranjan
General Secretary	Mr M. P. Sharma
Treasurer	Mr Rajeshwar Singh
Past President	Mr Krishan K. Chawla
Directors	Mrs Sandhya Bagwe
	Mr Gulshan Grover
	Mr Jivan Kayande
	Mr Prem Kharbanda
	Mr Surendra Kotak
	Mr Yogesh Kumar
	Mr Dhiru Bhai Ladwa
	Mr Vinod Marwaha
	Mr Mahendra Mehta
	Mr Gajanan S. Pundit
	Mr Rajiv Ranjan
	Mr Satish Sehgal
	Mr R. L. Singh
Auditors	Mr Rohit Desai

Appendix A: Past Executives and Boards

Mr Madan Prasad

2005–2006

President	Mr Preetam Sharma
VP Administration	Mr Amar Bhasin
VP Programs	Mrs Sandhya Bagwe
General Secretary	Mr Rajeshwar Singh
Treasurer	Mr Gulshan Grover
Past President	Mr Krishan Chawla
Directors	Mr Dhiru Ladwa
	Mr Gulshan Bhutani
	Mr Jivan Kayande
	Mr M. P. Sharma
	Mrs Niru Channan
	Mr Rajiv Ranjan
	Mr Ram Punjabi
	Mr R. L. Singh
	Mr Vasanti Patel
	Mr Vinod Marwaha
	Mr Yogesh Kumar
Auditors	Mr Rohit Desai
	Mr Mahendra Mehta

2006–2007

President	Mr Rajiv Ranjan
VP Administration	Mr Jivan Kayande
VP Programs	Mrs Sandhya Bagwe
General Secretary	Mr M. P. Sharma
Treasurer	Mr Gulshan Grover
Past President	Mr Preetam Sharma
Directors	Ms Nayha Acharya
	Mr Krishan Cahwla
	Mrs Niru Channan
	Mr Rohit Desai

	Mr Balwant Gandhi
	Mr Navdeep Girdhar
	Mr Mahendra Jain
	Mr Naresh Jha
	Mr Bharat Jobanputra
	Mr Yogesh Kumar
	Mr Madan Prasad
	Ms Shipra Seth
	Dr Ram Lakhan Singh
Auditors	Dr Krishan Katyal
	Mr Vipin Sharma

2007–2008

President	Mr Rajiv Ranjan
VP Administration	Mr Jivan Kayande
VP Programs	Dr Navdeep Girdhar
General Secretary	Mr Krishan Chawla
Treasurer	Mr Rohit Desai
Past President	Mr Preetam Sharma
Directors	Mr Rakesh Bansal
	Mrs Sandhya Bagwe
	Mr Sunil Channan
	Mr Jitendra Patel
	Mr Kiran Patel
	Mrs Charu Ranjan
	Mr Bijendra Singh
	Dr Rajeshwar Singh
	Dr Ram Lakhan Singh
	Dr Dinesh Rai
	Mrs Renu Narang
Auditors	Dr Krishan Katyal
	Mr Vinod Marwaha

2008–2009

President	Dr Rajeshwar Singh
VP Administration	Mr Amar Bhasin
VP Programs	Mrs Gunjan Sharma
General Secretary	Mr Krishan Chawla
Treasurer	Mr Gulshan Grover
Past President	Mr Rajiv Ranjan
Directors	Mrs Sandhya Bagwe
	Mr Rakesh Bansal
	Mr Gulshan Bhutani
	Mr Sunil Channan
	Mrs Jyoti Gupta
	Dr Krishan Katyal
	Mr Vinod Marwaha
	Mrs Poonam Mehra
	Mrs Renu Narang
	Mr Jitendra Patel
	Mr Shiv Saraswat
	Mr Arvind Sharma
	Mrs Achla Seth
	Mr Bijendra Singh
	Dr Ram Lakhan Singh
Auditors	Mr Madan Prasad
	Mrs Sarla Sharma

2009–2010

President	Dr Rajeshwar Singh
VP Administration	Mr Amar Bhasin
VP Programs	Mrs Gunjan Sharma
General Secretary	Mr Vinod Marwaha
Treasurer	Mr Krishan K. Chawla
Past President	Mr Rajiv Ranjan
Directors	Mrs Sandhya Bagwe
	Mr Vimal Bhatia

	Mrs Niru Channan
	Mr Gulshan Grover
	Dr Krishan Katyal
	Mrs Poonam Mehra
	Mrs Renu Narang
	Mr Jitendra Patel
	Mrs Charu Ranjan
	Mr Shiv Saraswat
	Mr Hiren Shah
	Mr Arvind Sharma
	Mr Preetam Sharma
	Mr Bijendra Sharma
Auditors	Dr M. K. Jain
	Mrs Sarla Sharma

2010–2011

President	Mr Jivan Kayande
VP Administration	Mrs Renu Narang
VP Programs	Mrs Charu Ranjan
General Secretary	Mrs Niru Channan
Treasurer	Mr Rohit Desai
Past President	Dr Rajeshwar Singh
Directors	Mr Arvind Sharma
	Mr Bijendra Singh
	Mr Bipin C. Chauhan
	Mr Kumud Acharya
	Mr Radhe Gupta
	Mr Sam Shah
	Mrs Savita Patel
	Mr Shiv Saraswat
	Mrs Shobhna Sharma
	Mr Surendra Sisodia
Auditors	Dr M. K. Jain
	Mrs Sarla Sharma

Appendix A: Past Executives and Boards

2011–2012

President	Mrs Renu Narang
VP Administration	Mr Amar Bhasin
VP Programs	Mrs Charu Ranjan
General Secretary	Mr Mahendra P. Sharma
Treasurer	Mr Kumud Acharya
Past President	Mr Jivan Kayande
Directors	Mrs Niru Channan
	Mr Bipin Chauhan
	Mr Varun Grover
	Mr Rajendra Harvi
	Mrs Savita Patel
	Mr Jitender Sahni
	Mr Shiv Saraswat
	Mr Arvind Sharma
	Mrs Shobhana Sharma
	Mr Bijendra Singh
Auditors	Mr Rohit Desai
	Mrs Sarla Sharma

2012–2013

President	Mrs Charu Ranjan
VP Administration	Mr Amar Bhasin
VP Programs	Mrs Savita Patel
General Secretary	Mrs Gunjan Sharma
Treasurer	Mr Kumud Acharya
Past President	Mrs Renu Narang
Directors	Mr M. P. Sharma
	Mr Shiv Saraswat
	Mrs Shobhna Sharma
	Mr Rajendra Harvi
	Mr Varun Grover
	Mrs Poonam Mehra
	Mr Gulshan Bhutani

Auditors	Mr Sanjay Sharma
	Mr Kiran Tawde
	Ms Bijenthi Mala Singh
	Dr Krishan Katyal
	Mr Subhash Surana

2013–2014

President	Mr Amar Bhasin
VP Administration	Mr Bijendra Singh
VP Programs	Mrs Savita Patel
VP Public Relations	Mr Rajeshwar Singh
General Secretary	Mrs Gunjan Sharma
Treasurer	Mr Varun Grover
Past President	Mrs Charu Ranjan
Directors	Mrs Renu Narang
	Mr Shiv Saraswat
	Mrs Shobhna Sharma
	Mr Rajendra Harvi
	Mrs Hansa Thaleshvar
	Mrs Poonam Mehra
	Mr Gulshan Bhutani
	Mr Sanjay Sharma
	Mr Kumud Acharya
	Mr Vinod Marwaha
Auditors	Dr M. K. Jain
	Dr Krishan Katyal

2014–2015

President	Mr Amar Bhasin
VP Administration	Mr Bijendra Singh
VP Programs	Mrs Gunjan Sharma
VP Public Relations	Dr Sanjay Sharma
General Secretary	Mrs Hansa Thaleshvar
Treasurer	Mrs Renu Narang

Appendix A: Past Executives and Boards

Past President	Mrs Charu Ranjan
Directors	Mr Kumud Acharya
	Mr Rajeev Arora
	Mr Gulshan Bhutani
	Mr Jignesh Gadhia
	Mr Vinod Marwaha
	Mrs Poonam Mehra
	Mrs Savita Patel
	Mr Shiv Saraswat
	Mrs Shobhna Sharma
	Mrs Anita Tripathi
Auditors	Dr K. Katyal
	Mr Madan Prasad

2015–2016

President	Mrs Gunjan Sharma
VP Administration	Dr Rajeshwar Singh
VP Programs	Mr Shiv Saraswat
VP Public Relations	Mr Rajeev Arora
General Secretary	Mrs Hansa Thaleshvar
Treasurer	Mrs Renu Narang
Past President	Mr Amar Bhasin
Directors	Mr Vipan Bansal
	Mr Gulshan Bhutani
	Mrs Kanak Chamarty
	Mr Jignesh Gadhia
	Mr Dhiru Ladwa
	Mr Savita Patel
	Mr Rajiv Ranjan
	Mrs Shobhna Sharma
	Mrs Rita Thapar
	Mrs Anita Tripathi
Auditors	Mr Kumud Acharya
	Mr Sarla Sharma

2016–2017

President	Mrs Hansa Thaleshvar
VP Administration	Mrs Renu Narang
VP Programs	Mr Shiv Saraswat
VP Public Relations	Mr Rajeev Arora
General Secretary	Mrs Charu Ranjan
Treasurer	Mr Vipan Bansal
Past President	Mrs Gunjan Sharma
Directors	Mr Gulshan Bhutani
	Mr Jignesh Gadhia
	Mr Manoj Kumar Gupta
	Mr Rajendra Harvi
	Mr Dhiru Ladwa
	Ms Chitra Omkar
	Mrs Savita Patel
	Mrs Shobhna Sharma
	Mrs Alli Soundararajan
	Ms Rita Thapar
Auditors	Mr Kumud Acharya
	Mrs Sarla Sharma

2017–2018

President	Mrs Hansa Thaleshvar
VP Administration	Mr Rajeev Arora
VP Programs	Mrs Charu Ranjan
VP Public Relations	Mr Manoj Kumar Gupta
General Secretary	Ms Chitra Omkar
Treasurer	Mr Vipan Bansal
Past President	Mrs Gunjan Sharma
Directors	Mr Kumud Acharya
	Mr Amar Bhasin
	Mr Gulshan Bhutani
	Mr Krishan Chawla
	Mr Rajendra Harvi

Appendix A: Past Executives and Boards 85

	Mr Desh Mitra
	Mrs Renu Narang
	Mrs Savita Patel
	Mr Shiv Saraswat
	Mrs Shobhna Sharma
Auditors	Mr M. P. Sharma
	Mr Jagdish Dalal

2018–2019

President	Mrs Savita Patel
VP Administration	Mr Rajeev Arora
VP Programs	Mrs Rita Thapar
VP Public Relations	Mr Manoj Kumar Gupta
General Secretary	Mrs Chitra Omkar
Treasurer	Mrs Renu Narang
Past President	Mrs Hansa Thaleshvar
Directors	Mr Ramesh Arjunaraja
	Mr Amar Bhasin
	Mr Gulshan Bhutani
	Mrs Charu Ranjan
	Mr Arvind B. Sharma
	Mr Preetam Sharma
	Mrs Shobhna Sharma
	Mr Govind Singh
	Mrs Artee Woosaree
Auditors	Mr Jagdish Dalal
	Mrs Anjali Agarwal

Appendix B: Notable Figures and Contributors

The Priests

Mr Sushil Kumar Kalia, Honorary Priest

Mr Kalia is the honorary priest of the HSA. He has been associated with the Society since 1976. Before Mr Dwivedi ji was appointed as priest, Mr Kalia performed most of the religious ceremonies for the HSA. Mr Kalia was born on January 1, 1940 in Ludhiana, Punjab, India. He studied at an Arya Samaj school. He completed a polytechnic engineering course before moving to Delhi, where he worked as an architect. Following this, he taught at the Industrial Training Institute in Delhi. Mr Kalia moved to England in 1966 for work, and began attending the Vedanta Centre in London. At that time, Swami Ghanananda was head of the Centre. Through the Vedanta Centre, Mr Kalia became acquainted with the works of Vivekananda and the Gospel of Sri Ramakrishna. He was most influenced by the teachings of Ramakrishna Mission, and was eventually initiated by Swami Ghanananda in Ramakrishna mantra. After Swami Ghanananda passed away, Swami Bhavyananda succeeded him. Upon the suggestion of Swami Bhavyananda, Mr Kalia created a Hindu religious organization called the Vedic Society of Southampton. He was also associated with Bharatiya Vidya Bhavan, which also influenced his religious outlook. He moved to Canada on March 1, 1976, spending a few weeks in Ontario before moving to Edmonton where he began work with a steel fabrication company. Mr Kalia introduced ritualistic activities at the HSA, worked on the construction of the HCC, served as President of the HSA for two terms (1985–1986 and 1998–1999), and organized interfaith dialogues. He still actively participates in the rituals at the HCC.

Acharya Shiv Shankar Prasad Dwivedi, Priest

Acharya Dwivedi was born on September 5, 1965. He was born and spent his early childhood in Atsalia, a remote village in Uttar Pradesh, India. In the absence of a formal education system, his mother laid the foundation of a pious upbringing. At the tender age of nine he lost his mother. When he was 13, he began studying Sanskrit and Ritualism at a gurukul in Naimisharanya. Eventually he became a student at Rishi Sanskrit Mahavidyalay founded by Rishi Keshavanand Maharaj, where he studied various intellectual disciplines (Sanskrit *śāstra*), historical and legendary literature (Sanskrit *purāṇa*), the *Rāmāyaṇa* and the *Bhagavadgītā*. Acharya Dwivedi studied Sanskrit at Sampurnanand Sanskrit University, Varanasi, receiving a gold medal for his efforts. He was also a recipient of a silver medal from the Ministry of Education, Government of India. In September 1989, he joined the HSA. In the same year, he established an educational institution in his native Atsalia where many students receive education as well as books and clothing free of cost.

Mr Yadav Ram Jha, Assistant Priest

Mr Jha was born into a Maithil priest family in Bhaktapur, Nepal on December 21, 1959. For many generations the family has taught Sanskrit and performed Hindu rituals in Nepal schools. Mr Jha completed his BA in Economics and Political Science, and then worked as a bank cashier from 1984 to 2009. He came to Edmonton in May 2009 with a work permit. His eldest sister Jaya Jha Corson sponsored him. In Edmonton he has conducted many Hindu religious ceremonies, especially those of the Nepali and Gahrwali Hindus. In 2015, Mr Jha studied English at the Northern Alberta Institute of

Technology (NAIT) after acquiring a study permit. In September 2016, he was appointed as an assistant priest by the HSA. His father late Tirtharam Jha volunteered as a priest in the Bharatiya Cultural Centre, Edmonton for many years.

First Committee Members of the HSA (1967–1968)

Dr Ram Krishan Gupta

Dr Gupta was the leading force behind establishment of the Society and was the first General Secretary of the same. Dr Gupta was born in 1927 into a poor grocer's family in a tiny village in the princely state of Narsinghgarh in central India. He received a state scholarship and completed his Master of Education at the University of Allahabad with first class standing. The Government of Madhya Bharat sent him to study in London from 1954 to 1956. There he received a master's degree in Educational Psychology. He then returned to India and worked as a professor at the University of Allahabad. He also worked as an administrator at Vikram University, Ujjain and then as a professor at Gorakhpur University. While he was in Gorakhpur, he received a research offer from University of Minnesota. He arrived there in 1960 and completed his PhD in 1965. Upon graduating, he joined the Faculty of Education, University of Alberta as an assistant professor, where he served until retiring as a professor in 1999. He was actively associated with the Society until his resignation from the Board in 1983. Dr Gupta's wife Indira Gupta was also one of the founding members of the Society.

Mr Gajanan Pundit

Mr Pundit taught in Ethiopia before coming to Canada in 1964. Once in Canada, he studied law at the University of Alberta.

He was called to the bar in 1971–1972, and then began his own practice. Since the inception of the Society, Mr Pundit has been an active member. He has also been involved with other cultural communities.

Mr Baldev Raj Abbi

Mr Abbi was a student member of the first committee of the Society and one of its founding members. He was a graduate student in Educational Psychology at the University of Alberta. Dr Gupta was a member of his thesis committee. Mr Abbi's wife Darshan Abbi was also a founding member. After Mrs Abbi passed away a few years ago, Mr Abbi moved to a seniors' home in Calgary.

Mr J. N. Sherman

Mr Sherman was a student member of the first committee of the Society. He was a Pashtun from the north-western province of India. He worked as a principal of the Hindu College in the territory of Nizam of Hyderabad. He was a schoolteacher as well as a part-time student at University of Alberta. He and his wife, daughter and son became founding members of the Society.

Mr Vidyasagar

Mr Vidyasagar was a student at the University of Alberta.

Signatories for the Document to Register the Hindu Society of Alberta under the Society Act (July 12, 1972)

Mr Uday Bagwe

Mr Bagwe was one of the early members of the Society and the General Secretary in 1972 after Dr Murdeshwar resigned from the post. His wife Mrs Sandhya Bagwe was also an active member. Mr Bagwe was born on January 26, 1936. He was a Maratha and was raised in Baroda. He became the curator at the museum of the University of Alberta. Later he opened a driving school. Many members of the HSA completed their driving lessons at his school. He played a major role in screening Indian movies, which was the most frequent activity of the HSA during its early days. In 2009, he moved to Calgary. Mr Bagwe passed away on March 10, 2010.

Dr Mangesh Ganesh Mrudeshwar

Dr Murdeshwar and his wife Mrs Maya Murdeshwar, a Maratha couple, were associated with the society from its inception. Dr Murdeshwar was born on March 25, 1933 in India. In 1961 he moved to Edmonton from Mumbai as a PhD student in the Department of Mathematics at the University of Alberta. He later became a professor there. He was the General Secretary of the Society for a short period in 1972. He was a vocal musician and performed Bhajans on numerous occasions. Dr Murdeshwar passed away on February 28, 2013.

Mrs Sunita Kumar

Mrs Kumar and her husband Prem Kumar were schoolteachers outside the city of Edmonton. Once they moved to Edmonton, Mrs Kumar became a homemaker, and Mr Kumar worked for the government. Mrs Kumar was a sitar player.

Mr M. P. Khandekar

Mr Khandekar was a meteorologist employed by the Government of Canada in the Department of Environment.

Mr S. Chakrabarty

Mr Chakrabartty was one of the founding members of the Society. He was born on April 9, 1928 in Rangpur in North Bengal. When he was 12 years old, his family moved to Uttarpara, a small town close to Calcutta. He did his schooling in Uttarpara and then completed his undergraduate studies in

Appendix B: Notable Figures and Contributors

Calcutta. He worked as a researcher with the Fuel Research Institute, Dhanbad before moving to the US in 1960 as a research student at Brandeis University. In March 1966, he was offered a position with the Alberta Research Council. He then came to Edmonton with his wife Aruna. Mr and Mrs Chakrabartty were actively associated with the Society from its inception. For many years Dr Chakrabartty served as an auditor for the board of the Society. He also stepped in to perform some religious rites when there was no priest in Edmonton. Mrs Chakrabartty taught Bengali as a part of language class program organized by the Society. Mr and Mrs Chakrabartty played a key role in the formation of the Vedanta Society of Edmonton, that operates out of the Hindu Cultural Centre.

Special Mention

Krishan Chandra Joshee

The Joshee family, comprised of Mr Joshee, his wife Karuna, and his parents Mrs Sumita Devi Joshee and Mr Arjan Das Joshee, were founding members of the HSA. Mr Krishan Joshee was born on March 19, 1923 in Lahore, Punjab, India and spent much of his youth between Lahore and his family village of Kathgarh. He moved to Canada in 1960 and taught public school in Spirit River, Alberta until 1967 when he and his family moved to Edmonton. He was a teacher with the Edmonton Catholic School Board until his retirement from that profession in 1985. Following his teaching career, he was Chair of the Alberta Gaming Commission and then Chair of the Wildrose Foundation. Outside of his work, he was an active volunteer who was recognized for his service to the community. He was a recipient of many honours and awards including the Order of Canada, the City of Edmonton Community Service Hall of Fame, and the Stars of Alberta. He was the first person of Indian origin to receive the Order of Canada, which recognized his work to promote multiculturalism and community development. Mr Joshee was actively associated with the Society at its inception and served as President of the HSA over four terms from 1974 to 1981. Mr Joshee was instrumental in introducing bingos and casinos through the Alberta Gaming Commission as sources of revenue for the Society. He also guided the application for major grants from the government. Mr Joshee passed away on February 25, 2014 in Edmonton.

Colophon: Typeset using the free, open-access typesetting system TeX written by Donald Knuth (XeLaTeX version), and the libre font Linux Libertine O from the multilingual Libertine Fonts collection.